May

Dear Mary Alice,

It was such a pleasure
talking with you the other night...
hard to believe its been 25
years! I hope we will do
a better job communicating.

I read once that "happiness is meeting
n old friend after a long time & feeling
that nothing has changed".

So true, my friend, so true.

Much love,

Honoring
The Legendary
Stanley E. Preiser

Stanley E. Preiser
1927 - 2009

TO VICTORY!

THE EXTRAORDINARY
LIFE OF
STANLEY E. PREISER

MONTY L. PREISER, J.D.
WEST VIRGINIA COLLEGE OF LAW

EDITOR
BLAIR T. PREISER, J.D.
VANDERBILT UNIVERSITY

outskirts
press

If I was on trial for my life and had to choose one lawyer to represent me, it would be Stanley Preiser
Roxanne Conlin, former President,
Association of Trial Lawyers of America

———◆———

Stanley Preiser's largeness is difficult for mere mortals to describe. He combined a physical presence of a tough athlete with the grace and intellect of a philosopher king
Richard Hailey, former President,
Association of Trial Lawyers of America

———◆———

A beautifully written work that describes with clarity and excitement not only the just portrayal of a legendary and selfless lawyer, teacher, and friend, but integrates the history of the trial bar during the mid to late 20th century. This was a book Monty Preiser had to write.
Gregg Rosen, retired partner McGuireWoods in Pittsburgh

TABLE OF CONTENTS

BEFORE THE BELL
Prologue

It may seem unusual to begin a biography with a eulogy. Yet I have seen many TV shows and films that begin with a funeral and flash back to the life of the subject.

In this instance, I think Rabbi Victor Urecki, our spiritual leader and friend from B'nai Jacob Synagogue in Charleston, WV, did a brilliant job of summing up the life of Stanley Preiser so that the reader will be eager to delve into the rest of this work and learn how and why Stanley earned these laudatory remarks. The Rabbi's observations help understand why over ten years after Stanley's death, the story of his exciting and significant life is worth learning.

December 19, 2009: Boca Raton, Florida, by Rabbi Victor Urecki

It is an honor to have been asked by Stanley himself to officiate today. Stanley Preiser and his family have always treated me with the utmost courtesy and kindness, and it is a privilege to be here. To Stanley's family and friends, I apologize in advance for these stumbling, halting words I am about to utter. But when the canvas of a human life has been filled with such vibrant colors and such varied texture, when the brush strokes applied have been both graceful and so elegantly beautiful, it becomes difficult to describe such a person adequately.

Stanley Preiser was a great and talented man, a magnificent voice in his chosen field. But he was more than a superb lawyer. His lifetime of achievements in the legal world lifted the entire profession to new heights and glory. Stanley Preiser was a brilliant man, but he was more than an intellect and scholar. He was a creative and imaginative genius that could take the impossible and make it a reality, the commonplace and elevate it to a standard by which all things are then measured. Stanley Preiser was a charismatic and dynamic human being, but he was more than that. He was a presence, an irrepressible force of nature, a gifted man of boundless energy, unmatched stamina, and complete commitment.

How does one capture such a man with words? How does one celebrate a life as spectacular as Stanley's in just a few minutes?

Well, Stanley Preiser was a proud member of the Jewish faith, and I think he would appreciate that I choose today to frame his life by noting the Jewish significance of the days of his passing and burial. Stanley passed away last Thursday, the 6th day of Chanukah, our Festival of Lights. It is the time we recall the victory of the Maccabees in ancient Israel. His date of passing also coincided with "Rosh Hodesh," the celebration of the new moon, an important monthly date on the Jewish calendar. And, finally, this day of Stanley's burial comes during the week where Jews read the story of Joseph and his brothers in Egypt.

In particular, the Torah portion which was read in synagogues this morning begins with our Patriarch Jacob's youngest son Benjamin falsely accused of thievery. He is unfairly incarcerated in Egypt, and it is Judah, the leader of the children of Israel, who passionately speaks out against this travesty of justice. He launches into one of the most powerful speeches in all the Torah, eloquently offering an incredible defense for Benjamin. His full throated and deeply moving plea in the court of Pharaoh moves Benjamin's jailer to tears and saves his life. I think Stanley would appreciate the fact that we read that section this morning. How appropriate!

Like Judah's defense of Benjamin, Stanley Preiser was, indeed, our defender, our eloquent voice, our Lion of Judah. Judah was unafraid to stand up in defense of the innocent. He was the only thing that stood between prison and freedom for Benjamin. And Stanley, too, was always ready to fight for the underdog, unwavering in the defense of cause or client, often the only thing that stood between the weight of injustice and his client's freedom.

Stanley was one of the most highly sought out lawyers in not only West Virginia, but beyond, throughout his memorable career. He was fully committed to defending the "little man," and earned his reputation as one of the best lawyers in the country. His skills, his oratory abilities, and his charismatic courtroom presence were unmatched. Stanley could outwork, out prepare, out maneuver, out think, and was better on his feet than any lawyer you would ever meet. I was told that of the 102 major criminal cases Stanley Preiser worked on, he won 99 of them, an unheard of percentage. This morning, Jews read how Judah won the day for Benjamin. Today, we pause and celebrate how Stanley always won the day for those who trusted him with their defense.

And he did it with more than just eloquence. Stanley did it with "presence." Stanley could walk in a room, freeze it, and own it. He entered a courtroom (or ballroom, or hall, or dinner reception) and people would turn, conversation would stop, and a crowd would gather.

I remember the first time I met Stanley Preiser. He and Joyce were already spending much more of their time and life in Florida. I had just started my career in Charleston and fortunately for me, Stanley was coming back to speak to our Men's Club. The topic they wanted him to discuss was "Capital Punishment," which was a big issue at that time in our state. Everyone was telling me how much I would enjoy meeting this larger than life man.

Typical of Stanley, he wasn't going to just speak about capital punishment from the legal angle. That would be easy. No, he wanted a challenge, and also wanted to play to the audience. The event was at the synagogue, so Stanley decided to explore the subject from the perspective of Jewish law. This wasn't going to be just a "surface" speech, something he would simply pull from a book or do off the cuff. As always, he plunged fully into the issue. Stanley exhaustively researched the topic — he called me weeks earlier, introduced himself over the phone, and wanted to pick my brain on a couple of sources he found in the Talmud (our Oral Law). And boy, did he know his stuff! I actually thought I was being cross-examined as the star witness for the prosecution. But I do recall thinking how captivating he was even on the phone, how charming and gracious, and how I couldn't wait to hear him.

And then I met him.

Nothing prepared me for my first encounter. Stanley came into the social hall of our synagogue. It was an experience I am sure many of you have seen, and I will never forget it. He entered and the room dynamics changed. His presence, that smile, that stance, that warmth; he lit up the room. And sure enough, and I saw this every time, and I am sure you did, too, everyone drew near to him; everyone came over to see him. And God bless him, he had everyone enthralled. He made sure we all knew he was glad to see us and he made each person feel special, whether by a hand on the shoulder, a warm embrace, a playful boxing jab, a knowing smile, or a personal quip. He could work a room. Why he didn't go into politics is beyond me!

And when he came up to me, he knew exactly what to say and how to make me, the new kid on the block in Charleston, feel special and immediately a part of his life. He looked pleased to see you and you, in turn, were honored to be in his presence. And that is what he brought to the courtroom. Stanley wasn't just brilliant of speech, but a powerful and charming persona.

And when he spoke, he could bend the course of a river.

I listened rather intently to Stanley that evening, and I saw why he was so successful. He impressed the hell out of me. He had mastered the subject he studied and prepared. His address could have been quite dry but it was one of the best prepared speeches on the subject I had ever heard. And he personalized it, reaching out to members of the audience, calling them by name, smiling at them. In fact, I remember during the speech he would look at me periodically and say, "Isn't that right, Rabbi?," "I think I have the Hebrew right, don't I Rabbi?," "Correct me if I am wrong, but I think the rabbi will agree with me…." He was one of a kind!

In both his questions and his answers, he *wanted* to be challenged, loved the back and forth debate, and I saw that intellect, that ability to think on his feet. And that is the way he was in the courtroom. Ready for anything, sharp, mesmerizing, and charming.

Like Judah who would not rest until Benjamin was safe, Stanley would use everything in his power, from preparedness to presence, determination to diligence, to defend his client. Like Judah, he would never abandon a defendant. How fitting, therefore, that Stanley's passing is today forever connected to Judah.

And how appropriate as well that Stanley's passing was on

Chanukah. The Maccabees were an outnumbered but courageous band who fought with a tenacity that liberated the homeland from the powerful, restored the Temple, and inspired a nation over 2000 years ago. Stanley was molded in their image. He said of himself when he was inducted this year into the American Trial Lawyers Hall of Fame, "I'm still tough as hell and mean as can be."

Tough indeed. He was a pit bull in the courtroom. Admired by his peers and feared by his opponents. Loved by those beside him or by those he promised he would stand to protect. He took incredible risks in the courtroom, fought hard, and wasn't afraid of anything or anyone. This former All State 2nd team football player for Charleston High, this eagle scout, this ex-boxer was a warrior — he never gave up, never backed down, never slowed down. He was as heroic as he was brilliant.

I said this to Stanley during these many months when he was suffering and when he told me his time was near: "Stanley, you are just too tough to give in." And I think he fought as long as he did, even while the pain may have made him want to quit, because he just didn't know how *not* to fight — and he was not going down *without* a fight.

Like the Maccabees, Stanley never gave in and never rested. Those who worked for him knew that when they came in at 7:30 AM in the morning, Stanley would already be there, and when they left at 10:30 PM, Stanley would still be there. He would return a call at *3:00 AM,* not to be a smart aleck, but because that was the first time he was free that day! And the unstated question was: "Why aren't *you* up, yet?"

Like the Maccabees, he lived life with dogged persistence and dedication; he was an irresistible force of nature. If you worked for Stanley, you had to be as willing and committed to the administration of justice and you had to work as hard and be as prepared for anything as he was. Not many could do that for long, but if you could keep up with Stanley, even for a short time, you learned a lifetime of experiences under this man. You studied under the best.

Studied under the best. As many told me, he wasn't just a great lawyer, but in the valued and cherished ideals of our faith, he was a great teacher. He taught young lawyers the skills they needed in this profession. You never finished a case with Stanley or, God help you, against him, without learning something. As much as he loved the courtroom, I think his world was the classroom. The courtroom was his chalkboard; he was the master and you, be you opposing counsel, jury, or judge, were the pupils. And Stanley enjoyed the relationship of guide and teacher to the next generation. He was a lawyer's lawyer. Like the Maccabees, Stanley was a courageous warrior, but like our people's finest heroes, a scholar and a teacher.

And, finally, Stanley was a loyal member of our religious heritage. The new moon is celebrated in our faith as a regular reminder of the uniqueness of our people. We base our holidays on the lunar calendar. The sun was celebrated by most cultures and so the Jews, perhaps to break away and proudly establish their own identity as a nation, used the moon as an affirmation of who we were and a pride in our separate identity.

Stanley always identified proudly with his people. Whether it was in raising his family in the importance of being Jews, or supporting such organizations as the Simon Wiesenthal Center and Federated Jewish Charities, identifying as a Jew was a source of pride for him. So was his family; he never forgot his roots, regularly sending contributions in the memory of his dear parents Joe and Madeline Preiser and extended family. When he became ill and couldn't come to Charleston for a visit, he would call and ask if I could go to the cemetery and say prayers at their gravesites on his behalf.

And B'nai Jacob Synagogue was important to him. He remembered my congregation in Charleston with frequent gifts, including most recently a new bima (altar); Stanley was proud of his people and proud to be a Jew. He never forgot where he came from, his roots, or his humble beginnings.

As a young lawyer starting out, many of the larger firms didn't want to hire this up and coming lawyer in Charleston. Why? Anti-Semitism. And Stanley made a promise to himself that when he made it and when he had his own practice, he would see to it that as much as he could his brethren would always have a place to start their careers in his firm. And he made good on that promise and brought many young Jewish lawyers to Charleston! And they in turn became great and respected lawyers in their own right for they had learned under the best. And thus, Stanley made our Jewish community a shining light, a source of strength and vibrancy.

Stanley Preiser, a proud and noble son of Israel. Like the celebration of the new moon, Stanley celebrated his Jewish identity.

Stanley Preiser gave dignity and strength to everything he did. His powerful stature, his captivating smile, his brilliance, his unparalleled work ethic and his boundless energy have all left lasting impressions upon us and everyone who ever met this man.

To his devoted wife Joyce, his son Monty and his wife Sara, to his daughter Terri, to his grandchildren Blair and Justin, these are just some of the gifts he has bequeathed to you. Celebrate today the gift God gave you in Stanley.

I end by saying blessed is the family that was given Stanley as a husband, a father and a grandfather. Indeed, blessed was our community who had the privilege of sharing his life. Because of Stanley

Preiser, we were in the presence of a Judah, a defender of the weak par excellence; we witnessed the heroism of the Maccabees, and like the moon, through him we always found light in the darkest of nights. Stanley's illuminating presence will shine with us all forever.

May his memory be for a blessing.

AMEN

AT THE BELL
May, 1976

The Defendant sat nervously in a small, makeshift room in the Federal Courthouse in Charleston, West Virginia. With him were his wife and two daughters, his lawyer, his lawyer's assistant just two years out of law school, and his lawyer's son, who would graduate from law school in two weeks. The conversation was aimless, stilted, and without much meaning – "killing time" as it were, while the group waited for the jury's verdict that would define the life of the Defendant from that day forward.

This was no ordinary trial. In fact, at that time it was the most watched trial in West Virginia history. The proceedings were covered by journalists and artists from every network and wire service in the country. Courtroom seating was limited, coveted, and controlled daily by United States Marshals interspersed throughout the courtroom to keep order. This was indeed no ordinary trial, for this was the first time in the annals of American justice that a sitting Governor had faced a trial on criminal charges.

Arch A. Moore, Jr. was a no-nonsense Republican Governor in what was then a heavily Democratic state. Prior to becoming Chief Executive six years before, he had served twelve years in Congress representing many of West Virginia's northern counties. He was funny, and gracious, but demanding, pompous, and sometimes exasperating. He was a good administrator who made forceful decisions and was clearly in charge of his state, but as Governor and the titular head of his party, Moore had many political enemies. One such adversary was the powerful *Charleston Gazette*, one of the state's two largest newspapers and a bastion of Democratic hate towards Moore. Nevertheless, he commanded enough respect, and could boast of enough accomplishments, that a positive legacy among the citizenry would have been assured but for the present trial.

The charge against the Governor was straightforward – according to the Federal Government Moore had accepted $25,000 in cash from Charleston businessman Theodore Price. In exchange, Price would receive a bank charter. The entire weight of the Federal Government was brought to bear for this prosecution, led by a supposed up and coming star, United States Attorney Jack Field. Representing the Governor was 49-year-old Charleston lawyer Stanley E. Preiser, already known in legal circles as a "lawyer's lawyer," and acknowledged nationwide among his peers to be one of the great trial lawyers of the day.

I have set out herein to tell the story of how Preiser rose to early prominence and maintained his lofty position for almost four decades. On the professional side, I have covered some of Stanley's most interesting and entertaining cases. You will hear input from lawyers who, throughout the years, have learned, litigated, and laughed with him, including myself. Of course, I was the law student mentioned at the start of this Prologue, and knew him better than anyone (short of my mother Joyce, and you will hear about her, too). From a unique and admittedly semi-biased perspective, I will also share some personal details of Stanley's private life, philosophy, and personality.

Lawyer or not, preferences for novels or biographies, I hope you will join me on a journey through the uniquely fascinating, often life impacting, sometimes humorous, and always uplifting, life of a truly extraordinary man. By the end, I expect you will understand why Stanley's favorite toast was always, as his family still toasts today: "To Victory!"

ROUND ONE

1927 – 1940

Prior to the early 1960's, before the Interstate system converged three major highways through the middle of its downtown, Charleston, West Virginia, was a sleepy, mostly unknown, relatively isolated state capital located at the western foothills of the Appalachian Mountains. Yet it was this isolation that allowed this small, highly white, Christian community to thrive, given that the roads were difficult, and sometimes impossible, to travel because they wound between the mountains that covered the vast part of the state.

In the early part of the 20th century, as railroads expanded and travel became easier, Charleston began to grow. New industries, including chemical, glass, timber and steel, migrated to the state, attracted by an abundance of natural resources such as coal and natural gas, as well as increased railroad availability. New construction seemed to be everywhere.

Along Kanawha Street, the area's primary throughway, sat the numerous mercantile stores that were run in great part by the city's minority population – the Jews, Italians, and Arabs. Out of necessity, members of these groups would find one another and form alliances to combat the rampant xenophobia then existing in this overtly southern town. Such exclusionary feelings would keep the small

African-American population openly segregated until the 1960's. More covertly, the immigrant groups were excluded from participation in many major parts of society, including large law firms, country clubs, and certain housing developments, until well into the 1970's.

This is the world into which Stanley Efrom Preiser was born on October 16, 1927. Stanley was the second son of Joseph and Madeline Levy Preiser, who, with Joe's sister Rose and brother-in-law Isadore, owned Davidson-Preiser, a thriving Dry Goods store located where the present Four Points by Sheraton hotel sits on what was Kanawha Street, and is now Kanawha Boulevard, a lovely and majestic divided four lane riverfront thoroughfare.

Stanley grew up in a home on Oney Street, located on the east side of the city where state government buildings now sit. The Capital Building, designed by the famed Cass Gilbert and widely considered one of the country's most grand, was completed in 1930. Young Stanley loved to explore or just hang out around the Capitol Building with its bucolic lawns and majestic view of the busy Kanawha River. His older brother Marvon (known as "Buddy") would often join him for those youthful excursions. Buddy, born in 1923, was four years older, and sadly passed away at the age of 57 in 1980. Stanley also had, and still has, a little brother, Jerome, but he was almost a full ten years younger, joining the family in June, 1937. Jerry later became a success in New York in both the music and culinary journalism fields.

Life as a child was one of relative ease for Stanley, even during the Depression years. Like most children who never knew anything else and were too young to understand the implications of the disaster, Stanley had no bad memories of the era. His father's store provided a solid middle class living, and, given the usual enclave of Jews who lived in the immediate area, during his first 13 years

Stanley experienced few of the problems and challenges of the outside world.

Gangster movies became the most popular film genre in the early 1930's. Invariably, they showed immigrants pulling themselves up by their bootstraps to become successful, even if that success was thanks to illegal means. There were so many murders, and so many kids who started to emulate the bad guys, that the League of Decency and Church leaders objected to the films. Responding, the movie industry quickly began featuring protagonists who were young, smooth, law-abiding heroes. The first picture of this type is generally regarded to be Warner Brothers' 1935 *G-Men*, starring James Cagney. It was a smashing success, and almost immediately other studios started pushing out films using the same formula. (Ironically, these new films promoting the good lawmen were just as violent as the old. This caused the British Board of Censors to threaten a ban on Hollywood film importation unless they were cleaned up. In response, Hollywood stopped making gangster pictures entirely for many years).

Stanley had been going to movies with his older brother Buddy since he was about seven years old. Growing up in this gun and violence culture, there is little doubt that he would have identified with hero James Cagney, who was fighting for the United States and for justice. Even as a child, Stanley was already thinking outside the box. In 1936, for example, he and his cousin Alvin Preiser, who was a year and a half younger and would be Stanley's life-long close friend, decided they would perform a particular civic duty.

The President of the United States, the great Franklin Delano Roosevelt, hero and icon to almost every West Virginian of the time, and certainly to every Jewish West Virginian, was coming to Charleston. Stanley and Alvin, being only 9 and 7 years old, naturally had no idea of how a President was protected, and so they decided to take on part of that responsibility themselves. Off they went to Stanley's father Joe's store and "commandeered" two BB guns. And up they went to the second floor of the building to "stand guard" with rifles at the ready as the great man motorcaded down the city's main street. There were no incidents, and the two boys went home that night content that they had served both God and country.

The neighborhood Jewish community on and around Oney Street had mostly immigrated from eastern Europe and Russia. As with most American Jews of that era, it was a struggle to keep one's Jewish identity in a highly Gentile world. Yet the Jewish parents of the 1930's tried. The community supported the traditional B'nai Jacob Synagogue, where Orthodox Jewish ritual and values were practiced until 2017, when the Congregation, in light of a dwindling Jewish population, joined the Conservative movement.

But in his formative years Stanley would, just as his children would 30 years later, attend Hebrew school from Monday through Thursday afternoons, pray at services on Saturday, and learn about his people in Sunday School. It was a full life when one remembers he was also in public school five days a week.

No indication exists, and no one ever claimed, that Stanley was a particularly good Hebrew or Sunday School student. There is evidence, however, that he was an all-around accomplished boy who chose to be part of the larger community around him. By the time of his Bar Mitzvah in 1940, Stanley had been captain of the patrol boys in 6th grade, achieved the highest level of the Junior Detective organization, and, perhaps most impressively, had become the youngest Eagle Scout in West Virginia history, receiving his special award in the Mayor's office in 1939. And his 5th grade marks in 1937 from Capitol Grade School foretold his success in college and law school:

A's in Reading, Spelling, Arithmetic, Geography, History, Music, and Physical Education. His only poor grades (and then only Cs) were in Art and Writing, the latter of which was understandable to everyone who knew and worked with him over the years. His penmanship never improved.

Whether a good Hebrew student or not, on the morning of his Bar Mitzvah, as with every 13-year-old boy at B'nai Jacob, Stanley was expected to stand before the entire Congregation and deliver a speech of some import. This was a special time in the life of the Congregation as it had just finished observing Yom Kippur, the highest holy day of the year. What is probably Stanley's first foray into public speaking still exists in his handwriting, which is, surprisingly, quite readable. Most importantly, these words seem in fact to foreshadow much of the philosophy by which Stanley would live his adult life as well:

Worthy Rabbi, Dear Teachers, Beloved Parents, Relatives, and Friends:

On this long-awaited Sabbath day when I stand here in the Synagogue about to be admitted into the ranks of our people, there are two thoughts that are uppermost in my mind. First is my expression of gratitude to my parents.

My dear parents, I know you have waited a long time for this day when you could see me become Bar Mitzvahed and except [sic] the faith of my people. I want to tell you today that I appreciate your every kindness to me through all these years. I know how much you are constantly sacrificing for me, as only parents do. I realize how much of your lives you spend in caring, working, and planning for me and my future. I know how ready you are to endure any hardship for my welfare. Everything that I have and enjoy comes through your devotion to me.

Of course, I should show my feelings of appreciation every day of the year. But, if at times I have brought you sorrow when I should have given you joy; if in the passed [sic] I have caused you regrets when I should have brought happiness; if I have been disobedient and disrespectful when I should have fulfilled your every wish, I want you to forgive me. I hope that in the future I shall be able to make you feel truly proud of me. I am thankful to God that he gave you to me, and from now on I hope to be deserving enough to have you say the same about me.

The second thought that passes through my mind on this long-awaited day of my Bar Mitzvah concerns the path of duty that lies ahead of me. A Jewish boy has many obligations he must fulfill to rightfully earn the name Jew. On rising in the morning, he must don his Tefillan [Author's Note: phylacteries] and recite the prayers to affirm his faith in God and in his people. The Jewish holidays should be days that will bind him to the glorious past of Israel. Likewise, most all other customs and practices should form a part of his Jewish life.

Nor can a truly Jewish boy forget his duties to his fellow man. His conduct at school, at home, or on the street must always be honorable. To be the gentleman and never the ruffian must be his motto at all times. To all these duties I pledge myself on this day of my Bar Mitzvah.

I pray to God that he bless my dear parents, grandmother, relatives, and friends with years and years of life and health. I now take the path of duty that will enable me to grow up to be a Jew in name, in honor, in thought, and in action.

Amen.

It is difficult to charge a young man of 13 to model his adulthood on a pledge made in a house of worship. Yet there are hints in what Stanley wrote that suggest he took his own words seriously. Throughout his life, the respect he showed his parents, his wife, his children, and his friends was a vital part of his day. My father once told me, after I had not been particularly respectful to him one afternoon as a teenager, about he and my grandfather when Stanley went to purchase his first house. Apparently, Joe knew very little about property or modern housing, but Stanley said he no sooner would have bought a house without asking his father's advice than he would have jumped off a tall bridge! To Stanley, that was respect. And he showcased that quality until his death. Unless, of course, he felt strongly that someone did not deserve it.

The other part of the Bar Mitzvah speech that seems to have molded Stanley was the promise to be honest, a gentleman, and never a ruffian. Translate ruffian into "bully," and you have the underlying dedication of his life. Whether he tried civil or criminal cases, whether someone simply asked him for help, or whether he sought out injustice, Stanley Preiser was on the side of the underdog, the downtrodden, the weak, and the disadvantaged.

Who knows whether all of this resulted from a 13-year-old's first speech, or whether that speech and all that followed were the result of his upbringing? Or perhaps his innate character? Perhaps both. But the cause is often less important than the effect, and in this case the effect was a kind of real life super hero. Naturally, Stanley did not have any supernatural powers, but one would have to look far and wide to find someone who would dispute that whatever it was he did possess was nothing less than magical.

ROUND TWO
1941 – January 26, 1944

Stanley finished Junior High School in the Spring of 1941. Though only approaching age 14, he looked 3-4 years older. While many of America's young men were already in uniform, and after Pearl Harbor in December only a few would be able to escape the call, 14-year-old Stanley looked like an 18-year-old civilian. This was not the best image to present in time of war, and invited inevitable insults from those who believed he should be serving. The resultant fights against such older competition were difficult for Stanley to win.

Not that he was a weakling. As with most Jewish boys post-Bar Mitzvah, Stanley began spending less time at the synagogue, and more time with his friends. With perhaps too much free time after school, he and many of his Jewish, Italian, and Arab friends spent their Junior High years in numerous scuffles with gentile boys who weren't too happy about recent immigrant minorities invading "their" turf, attending "their" schools, learning from "their" teachers, and so on. But Stanley, who would enter Charleston High School in the fall, was determined to build himself up so he could handle whatever physically came his way.

Stanley began frequent trips to the YMCA's weight room, and they were paying off big time. He became a 1940's hunk – a real American beefcake. He joined the high school football team, and though he mostly rode the bench in 1941, he learned the game. His friends from those years often regaled me with stories of Stanley's strength, agility, and tenacity. There were not many who dared go against him one on one, or even two to one. Occasionally Stanley and a couple of friends would take on an entire rival football team, and existing pictures are testimony to the fact that no one came out a winner.

Almost any friend of Stanley's will tell you the legendary stories of how he would challenge anyone to hit him in the stomach as hard as they could. It became an expected challenge and, incredibly, until his late 70's his workout program allowed him to absorb every punch I ever saw him take.

On Sunday, December 7, 1941, Stanley and his friends were in a movie theatre when the film was interrupted with the announcement of the Japanese attack on Hawaii. Like most Americans, he had never heard of Pearl Harbor, but was enraged and energized by the thought of a foreign country attacking the American navy in a secret raid. It wasn't long before Stanley's patriotism and machismo had him at the enlistment office lying about his age so he could join the army.

It is likely that the government was so concerned with readying for war (the United States was ill-prepared to fight) that it enlisted hundreds of kids without verifying their ages, and sent them off to combat too soon. But early service was not in the cards for Stanley. Madeline Preiser was too smart and too protective of her son to let that happen. Upon somehow learning of Stanley's plans, she hustled down to the enlistment location to give the officer in charge a piece of her mind. Needless to say, Stanley did not enter the armed forces in 1941, and he was not yet 18 when the conflict ended in August of 1945.

The first half of 1942 was nation-wide chaos as the United States geared up for all-out war. The Depression was over, women joined the work force in great numbers to replace the men who were now away, and stores were open late to accommodate the non-stop production that would ultimately prove to be too much for the Axis powers to overcome. What all this meant for Stanley was that his parents were not home very much. He would periodically work in his father's dry goods store during the day, where he received an education in selling and its attendant psychology, and then join his friends for all-night parties that did not always end in a peaceful manner.

By the summer of 1942, however, a more disciplined Stanley had determined that football was indeed for him. He was innately smart, and had become powerful and wrestler-quick, a perfect combination for a lineman who played both offense and defense. His participation on the school football team immediately brought to the front many lasting personality traits. As we saw from his Bar Mitzvah speech, they were probably already ingrained, and included his desire to be the best, and to employ every legitimate, available tactic to win.

After attending the Boy Scouts of America leadership camp and penning the camp newspaper's sports column, it finally came to pass that in the fall of 1942 a not-yet 15-year old Stanley Preiser suited up as a starting tackle for the mighty Charleston High School Mountain Lions. He quickly built a reputation as one of the team's leaders and best linemen in the State, often referred to by Charleston sports writers as "Dependable" or "Rough and Ready." His fearlessness was noticed and commented on by reporters and opposing teams alike. Safety equipment, unfortunately, was not what it is today. Leather helmets lacked face guards and did not provide adequate protection. So, while "His Boldness" may have won football games, it also scored him numerous broken noses and ear injuries that would trouble him for the rest of his life.

The end of the 1942 football season did not slow Stanley down. It became fashionable after Stanley gained notoriety in adulthood for many friends to not-so-jokingly quip that they never saw him during high school (his senior picture was not, for example, in the year book), thereby implying he may have been something of a slacker once football responsibilities were completed.

However, the records and newspapers do not bear out these myths, and by all accounts Stanley was incredibly busy in the first 8 months of 1943. He followed the war news carefully as the tide turned in favor of the Allies. January saw the first uprising of the Jews in the Warsaw Ghetto, the first bombing of Berlin, and the Casablanca Conference where Roosevelt and Churchill planned the invasion of Europe. Soon thereafter the Germans surrendered at Stalingrad, the Allies in the Pacific began their March to Japan, and the Germans began to murder communities of Jews.

At home, life continued, and Stanley was determined not to miss much of it. His January grades, while not the marks he once received, and would later earn again, were anything but poor – A's in Biology, History, and Phys Ed, a B in Chemistry, and a C in English. He also found time not only to play in the statewide AZA (Aleph-Zadek-Aleph, an international organization for Jewish teenagers) basketball tournament, but was honored as all-tournament while helping lead his team to the championship. When not suited up and on the court, Stanley served as manager of the high school basketball team, and, to the surprise of all of those researching this book, he was also runner up in the Chemical Gardens category of the school flower show (this involved an experiment usually performed by adding metal salts, such as copper sulfate or cobalt chloride, to a solution of sodium silicate. This result is the growth of plant-like forms in minutes to hours).

Autumn of 1943 saw the surrender of Italy and the Allies subsequent invasion of that country to drive out the Germans. It also promised one of the best Mountain Lion football teams in years, and Stanley was firmly anchored as one of the state's best players, earning 2nd Team All-State honors at the end of the year. In those days the Charleston papers regularly covered high school sports on a much greater level than one might imagine now. They were full of accolades for Stanley and the team.

One major story and one unique event marked this 1943 season. The anecdote came directly from Nathan Yerrid, a long-time friend of Stanley's, and sometimes his back-up at tackle. It seems Stanley had a reputation for giving the player across the line from him a pretty rough time. It was also unusual for Stanley to ever leave the game. However, on November 25th Stanley and Stonewall Jackson lineman Bob Cunningham were ejected from the game for, the newspaper says, "becoming a little too ambitious." Poor Nathan, as he told the tale, was substituted in for Stanley. When he entered the game the Stonewall players glared at him as if he were a sacrificial lamb upon whom they could exact some pretty heavy revenge for Stanley's actions toward them. Nathan would finish the story by saying that he changed positions the very next day.

As for the alluded to "event," on Wednesday, October 6th, the newspaper broke the story that "rugged tackle" Stanley Preiser would be unable to play on Friday night the 8th because it was Yom Kippur Eve, the holiest night on the Jewish calendar. This was an especially tough blow to Stanley and the team because the opponent, Parkersburg High, was Charleston's most serious challenger for the state championship. Stanley was pretty devastated, not so much for his own glory, but because he did not want to let down his friends. To be attending services that Friday night instead of attending to his quarterback was not what he had envisioned. And so, it was not what he planned.

The night of the Parkersburg vs. Charleston football game was a wet and chilly Yom Kippur eve. 5,000 miles away the U.S. 8th Air Force sent 378 B-17s and B-24s on a bombing raid deep inside Germany for the first time, surprising the Nazis. And in Charleston, reliable old number 68 was indeed nowhere to be found – either on the field or in the synagogue.

So, who was that number 71 (Stanley was 66 or 68) knocking back the defense and making more than his share of tackles? None other than Stanley, who had swapped jerseys with, and was playing under the name of, Bob Hess. One assumes this was done with at least his coach's knowledge, but Stanley never snitched. The end to the story? After a sterling first half he injured his leg on the first play of the second half and was laid up for a few weeks, thereby missing 2 future games. Fate? Something more? Or just coincidence?

As to the game itself, Parkersburg prevailed and, as West Virginia's only undefeated team that year, was voted state champion by the West Virginia sportswriters. Princeton was runner up, and the Mountain Lions ended up in third place. An honored position, but not what they had hoped.

At 7:00 a.m. on January 17, 1944, the day after General Dwight D. Eisenhower assumed command of the Allied Expeditionary Force which would spearhead the invasion and liberation of Europe, a recently turned 17-year-old Stanley Preiser received his high school diploma during a small mid-year graduation ceremony in the high school auditorium. Nine days later, while 500 bombers hit

Berlin, Stanley received a telegram informing him that he had been awarded the Laverne Noyes Scholarship for his subsequent admission to the prestigious University of Chicago, and he had only five days until orientation.

ROUND THREE

January 31, 1944 – June, 1950

The University of Chicago is one of the premiere research and academic institutions in the world, ranking in the top 10 in most rated categories, and boasting campuses in London, Paris, Delhi, Beijing, and Hong Kong, as well as downtown Chicago.

In 1944, the University and the city of Chicago were jumping places to be. Only thirteen months prior to Stanley's arrival in Chicago, the University's metallurgical laboratory produced the world's first man-made self-sustaining nuclear reaction beneath, of all places, the stands at the school's Stagg football stadium. Not too long before that, the same lab was the world's first to isolate plutonium. Both discoveries were critical to the Manhattan Project – the creation of the Atomic Bomb. Chicago, being second only to Detroit in value of war goods produced, was a progressive town and indeed one on the rise. It was becoming home for 60,000 African-Americans escaping the Jim Crow South, and the same number of Japanese-Americans who had been released from the shameful desert internment camps.

Stanley arrived in this hustling, bustling city, effectively on his own for the first time. He had traveled with his parents to Miami Beach and New York City, and so was not a total stranger to big city ways, but doing it alone, and for a long period of time, would be truly a new experience. His immediate need was for spending money. Although he was on partial scholarship and his parents had funds to make him comfortable, like any young man on the move Stanley needed some disposable income. He was still competing with servicemen in uniform for the ladies, and extra pocket money would help him keep his dates fed, and his snappy wardrobe up to snuff.

Stanley possessed three awe-inspiring attributes that would serve him well in life. First, he had an almost photographic memory that worked in conjunction with an orderly mind that could "see" steps ahead of most any situation in which he found himself. With these abilities he flourished as a card and chess player, and eventually found himself playing Bridge and chess for money throughout his college career. He was as successful at those endeavors as he would be with everything else in his life.

Second, Stanley had boundless energy. He lived the first 60 years or more of his life rarely sleeping more than five hours a night, yet continually functioning at an amazingly high level. He always said he lived at least an extra life time with the three additional hours he spent awake every day while the rest of the world slept.

Third, Stanley's strength and agility gained from all that time working out at the YMCA gym, as well as his proclivity for hard work and study, made him a more than passable boxer. Mix in some mental toughness from his early street fighting, and you have the "guy you stay 3 rounds with and win a prize" at the local carnivals. Here, he could make some money. Stanley did have one cardinal rule. He told it to me in later years while teaching me to box and fight. It was, "If anyone ever hit me hard enough to knock me down, I stayed there."

[Author's Note: Stanley would continue to watch professional boxing throughout his life. Except for golf, he didn't really follow any other sports. Boxing may be the only sport (save perhaps weightlifting) where there has been little to no performance enhancing equipment created since the days of James Corbett. Track, swimming, football, baseball, tennis, etc., all have clothing, shoes, or equipment designed to make one go faster, jump higher, hit farther, or catch easier. But boxing was the same, and one can understand why Stanley, who took no time for TV or team sports, would have clung to that sport.

Long after law school, Stanley worked with, and in some cases represented, the Cleveland group that opened Caesar's Palace in Las Vegas in 1966. He loved the game of Craps and was almost a legend at trial lawyers' meetings held in casino cities. He could play for hours, pretty large stakes, and crowds would watch and cheer. In later years, if the whole family happened to be in Vegas or Atlantic City together, more than once I was awakened at 3:30 a.m. by my mother, who asked me to go downstairs and "invite" my dad to come to bed. Sometimes it even worked.

On January 27, 1973, Dad took me to Las Vegas for my first time (though I wasn't yet 21, the drinking age in New Orleans during college at Tulane was 18, and so I was prepared). We went to see the United States vs. Soviet Union International Boxing Championship. Most of what I recall is that we had an invitation through Dad's friends for a private party at the top of Caesar's with the Soviet boxers, who were all close to my age. They were allowed to chat a little bit, and those who spoke English were amazed at the United States. If you ever visited the Soviet Union before the "Wall" came down, you will know why. They had nothing. I also recall that during the matches themselves, the

*U.S. crowd was calling for blood. Relations with the USSR were
not too cordial in the early 70's.]*

But back to 1944. Two years in Chicago went relatively quickly
and easily. Stanley earned excellent grades and had as much nightlife
as one man can stand – with a date or two on his arm he frequent-
ed sporting events and jazz bars — where he could always drink a
prodigious amount of spirits. As a rule, the spirits made him jovial
and nice, but cross him in any way and he could become mean and
potentially dangerous to the offending party's health. Fortunately,
those were rare occurrences.

The War ended in Europe in the spring of 1945, just as the
year's second semester was complete. Stanley would enroll at the
University of Virginia in the Fall, a highly respected school located
in the beautiful town of Charlottesville. Until I began writing this
book, the reason for the move was never clear, and my Dad was un-
characteristically vague when I asked.

However, I finally discovered through an almost unimpeachable
source why Stanley left Chicago. Apparently, he was being stalked
by a woman he had dated who insisted on marriage. Stanley was unable to "shake" her, so he left a message for her that he was going to
die, and went East. She had no idea where he went, so that was that.
As I contemplated this explanation, it did not seem so fantastical, for
after Stanley gained notoriety, occasionally deranged people would
call him for days on end. He finally just instructed the receptionist
to tell them he was dead. Surprisingly, the calls usually ceased. It isn't
clear why this worked, but follow-up and fact checking were not as
easy then as in the "Google Age."

The first few years after the War brought great changes to the
entire country, and Stanley was not immune. People wanted to

forget the darkness of conflict, and frivolity became more the norm. This was especially true at a southern school with a party reputation already in place. As soldiers returned from abroad, they took advantage of the GI Bill and filled the colleges in the land with men who had seen the world and the horrors of war, and were also 2 - 4 years older than other University students. Partying and entertainment began to look and mean a little different than before. Radical shifts were being made in dating and relationships as well.

Women had been out of the house performing what had traditionally been designated as men's jobs, and they weren't ready to so easily give up their new-found freedom and independence. And the country had money – the work force had put away tremendous amounts of savings because rationing had given them few places to spend for four years. Now, this money was buying products, dining, and other night life. When Stanley first got off the train in Charlottesville, this "New America" was there to greet him.

Most of the stories one hears about Stanley at Virginia revolve around women, card games, alcohol, and fun. Legend has it the prankster once put a live cat in a friend's biology cadaver bag at midnight on Halloween. There are numerous pictures from those years to back up the stories. The women are good looking, the guys have silly grins and look a little disheveled, and some great dice games are memorialized. Looking at these photos, one can almost feel the excitement and zeal springing forth from these young men.

A discovered newsletter identifies "J. Edgar Preiser" as the head G-man of the FIB ("Fun in Bed"), appointed as such after taking care of 39 cases in six months. Said Stanley in a faux interview, "I am going to delegate a portion of my cases to my associates, but will continue to handle the more difficult ones myself."

Despite all of that nonsense, a newspaper blurb from Charleston announced that Stanley made the Dean's Honor Roll during his first semester, which ended in early 1946 (his report card shows an A in Sociology 5, and B's in Economics 1, Mathematics 2, Psychology 2, and Rural Social Economics). Good marks would continue, and improve, until his graduation with a B.A. in 1947, and his acceptance to law school at the University of Louisville. There, in Kentucky, his life was destined to change indelibly.

When 19-year old Stanley Preiser first drove into Louisville in August of 1947, he was a study in contrasts. Suits were the uniform of the times in law school, while he spent what leisure time he had usually dressed in a rakish, but stylish, leather bomber jacket. As his appearance was always foremost on his mind, and as he was a perfect size 38, he could easily buy off the rack. The following story associated with this was confirmed by more than one person.

Recall that Stanley's father Joe owned a dry goods store in Charleston where they sold, among other things, shoes, work clothes, and suits. The day before Stanley first drove to Louisville, he "borrowed" 10 suits, and then wore a different one each day in class. Imagine the stir he caused the first two weeks. But the story is far from finished. At the end of the two weeks, and most every two weeks after that, he would pack up the suits and drive the 7-8 hours to Charleston (the drive with Interstates is now less than 4 hours), put the suits back on the rack, take ten new ones, and off he would travel back to Kentucky where students and faculty alike would continue to marvel and be flabbergasted at his perceived wardrobe.

The reverse would never have been true, however, as envy was not something one could pin on Stanley. In the same vein, he didn't care to hear people comment or complain about how much someone else had and/or lacked. He would dismiss this type of discussion with a quick declaration that, "Someone always has a bigger boat."

During his entire trial career, one rarely saw Stanley in or near a court house without his being impeccably dressed and driving an expensive car. It was more than vanity. As with most of his actions, he had a reason: "The jury should know the client has an expensive and successful lawyer. They will award more money and everyone wants to associate with a winner."

That being the usual play, there were some exceptions, mostly when Stanley was in a major city. Depending on the circumstances he might dress like the locals (cowboy boots) or dress down so hot-shot New York lawyers and juries would underestimate him at first. Whatever he chose, I never knew him to fail at trial.

In those days at U of L Law School, apparently grades were only given at the end of the year. Stanley's first report card in June of 1948 reflects A's in Torts and Land Use, and B's in Constitutional Law, Criminal Law, and Contracts. But Stanley was seriously distracted during the early part of 1948. That distraction came in the lovely form of Joyce Monfried, 19-year old daughter of Bernard "Ben" and Rose Monfried of Louisville.

Ben was an optometrist who founded Monfried Optical, which would become one of the largest optometry chains in the country (though he had to put up with Stanley's everlasting ribbing because he sold it before that major expansion occurred and before there was any real money). Rose was at one time a concert pianist. They parented four pretty daughters (including Joyce), and in the way of the times taught them the arts of matrimony and motherhood.

Joyce always claimed to have played the violin, though I never heard it. She did, however, sing well enough to entertain at local USO functions during the War when she was 14 and 15 years old. It was through Joyce that her children both inherited their love of (and any small talent that might exist in) music, theatre, and entertainment.

Stanley had seen Joyce around campus, and had started hanging out near her house, to the consternation of Ben and Rose who finally, and exasperatedly, demanded of Joyce, "Who is the hood in the leather jacket, anyway?" Joyce, the story goes, made it known to Stanley that she simply was not interested. Her sisters always told me that was not true.

Then one night it happened — Father Irony came to town. Joyce was visiting a girlfriend's apartment and had left a note on the apartment door of a law student she knew (call him Bill). The note asked if Bill would escort her home later that evening. As "luck" would have it, Stanley and Bill were out together that evening and when they returned to Bill's place, Stanley saw the note. He took it and rang the bell of the apartment where Joyce was visiting. When she answered the door, Stanley tore the note up and dropped it in her hand. Well, Joyce was not then, nor would she ever be, a shrinking violet. In no uncertain terms she informed Stanley that he would be the one to see her home. He did, and a life-long love story was born.

Joyce and Stanley's wedding took place at the Daniel Boone Hotel in Charleston on September 6, 1948. After a short honeymoon in Manhattan, it was back to school, where Stanley was now focused on his classes, career, and wife.

His grades at the end of 1949 showed A's in Trial Practice, Trusts, and Creditor's Practice, a B in Family Law, and a surprising C in Corporations. He was, however, appointed by the faculty to the Board of the "Briefing Service," a high honor. More often than not, when he received an A his was the top grade of the class in both 1949 and 1950. As a matter of fact, Stanley's 1950 report card shows all A's in Trade Regulations, Partnerships, Insurance, and Wills. At least until his death, Stanley's average score that year was reputed to be the highest in school history.

[Author's note: Stanley also earned high marks in the family department. For all his hard and dedicated work throughout the years, his family was always the most important, most proud, and happiest part of his life. I remember in April of 1991, Stanley took Joyce, my wife Sara, and me to Atlantic City to witness the "Battle of the Ages" between Evander Holyfield (who was owned by some friends of Stanley's in Florida) and George Foreman (pre pitchman days). Dad had no legal meetings, we had close to ringside seats near Kevin Costner, and the fight went all 15 rounds, with Round 7 being voted as one of the great boxing rounds in history. Holyfield won by decision, but it didn't really matter. Dad was with family during one of the rare times before he retired that I saw him truly enjoy three days of doing just what he wanted to do. And it was something.]

ROUND FOUR
July, 1950 – May, 1951

Stanley passed both the Kentucky and West Virginia Bar Exams with little trouble during the summer, which was fortunate because he had already made up his mind to further his education by pursuing a Masters of Tax Law at New York University. So, immediately after his admission to the West Virginia Bar on September 15, 1950, he and Joyce moved into a small apartment on East 18th St. in Brooklyn, where they shared a kitchen and bath with another couple. The four of them did not get along very well. Fortunately, the Preisers were not often at home.

Stanley spent much of his time in the library with his nose in the books, while Joyce worked on Broadway and 7th St. at Wanamaker's, then one of the leading department stores in the world with over 32 acres of retail space (it closed in 1955). Yet Stanley, at not quite 23 years of age, was already Stanley. He had an idea that he thought could earn them enough money in three months to truly enjoy New York until he graduated in June. And, as usual, he was proven right.

So it was that on October 1, 1950, Stanley and Joyce opened their own toy store. Stanley's classes were in the morning, so he ran the operation in the afternoons (they opened at 1:00). Joyce would handle the evening shift from 5:00-9:00 while Stanley studied. There were, naturally, hundreds of toy stores in the Tri-State area, especially leading up to Christmas and Chanukah. But Stanley had undertaken meticulous research to determine what the most popular items of the year would be. He stocked up and charged 50% to 60% higher for them than anyone in the area. At those prices, the toys didn't sell very well in October and November, but when the other retailers were sold out in December, Stanley and Joyce became the only game in town and, as the saying goes, they "cleaned up."

The rest of the school year was indeed as enjoyable as planned. In the city that truly never slept, they had time after classes, study, and work for cocktails, dinner, and nightclubs, things they both loved and (for better or worse) passed on to me.

Joyce loved music, and one of the great evenings of her life occurred soon after she and Stanley opened the toy store. Judy Garland had been Joyce's idol ever since *Wizard of Oz* premiered in 1939, and Joyce's dream was to see Judy perform in person. She saw her chance to make this wish come true when Stanley happened to have an upcoming birthday on the very night Judy was to open her show at the Palace. Joyce, who always maintained with a wink that she meant the surprise to be for Stanley's birthday, presented him with two tickets to Judy's opening night.

That concert is considered by many to be the finest of Garland's storied career. Growing up, I must have listened to the LP recording of that performance a hundred times or more.

That isn't to say Stanley was not a music fan of sorts, though he preferred western and biographical films in his free time. His idol was Al Jolson, who is still considered by many to have been the greatest entertainer of all time, and who starred in the film *The Jazz Singer*. It was released the year of Stanley's birth, and is often incorrectly credited as the first talking picture. Stanley's love affair with Jolson started in 1946 when he took a date to see *The Jolson*

Story, starring Larry Parks, in Charlottesville. He was hooked, often watching the film 3 times in a day.

My earliest recollection of Jolson was as a first grader when I would be awakened each morning by Dad crooning (Bing Crosby, he wasn't) one of Jolson's great hits, *Carolina in the Morning*, or, just to change things up a bit and prove he knew other performers, Rodgers and Hammersteins's *Oh, What a Beautiful Mornin'* from the show *Oklahoma*. Jolson music, however, was the soundtrack of Dad's efforts to relax, and by the time I went to college in 1969, I could sing a pretty fair rendition of every song. I also knew the words and music to most every successful Broadway musical and Garland song, as those were Mom's downtime preferences. But, back to Jolson. Stanley's fascination with him endured throughout his entire life. He served as President of the International Al Jolson Society, on more than one occasion engaged the finest Jolson impersonator in the land to entertain at one of his private parties, and even left instructions in his will that after his funeral those attending the luncheon should enjoy themselves listening to Jolson music.

For all the fun the couple had in New York, Stanley still graduated with his Masters in May of 1951. The next chapter of the Preisers' life had begun: it was time to establish a career and earn a living.

ROUND FIVE

June 1951 – June, 1954

It isn't clear whether Stanley always intended to begin his practice in West Virginia, given that he had chosen to go to Kentucky for law school, and then married a Kentucky girl who had three sisters and a slew of cousins in Louisville. But, just as Joyce had support in Kentucky, Stanley had family and roots in Charleston, West Virginia, including *more* than a slew of cousins – his father was one 9 children and his mother one of 6, most, if not all, of whom were still Charleston residents in 1951. And while my Kentucky cousins will not like reading this, Dad always felt Charleston, as the state capital, offered more action and had more to do than Louisville ever did. And I believed him – which is why my cousins' semi-playful ribbing about being a West Virginian probably never bothered me.

For whatever reason, the Preisers selected Charleston, and moved into Stanley's childhood home on Oney St. in late 1951, where Stanley prepared to start his practice, and Joyce prepared for a new arrival: me, born in Charleston on May 2, 1952.

Charleston in the 1950's was becoming a pretty wide-open town. Just as Prohibition had spawned a nightclub and backroom culture nationally a generation before, Kanawha County, like most of West Virginia, was dry. To enjoy spirits, one had to belong to a private club. Most of these establishments were operated by people with ties to the criminal element, but they were smart enough to involve leading citizens as investors. In a word, the clubs provided a lot of action — some legal and some not. This would be the norm until well into the 1980's in Charleston. Add the legislators and their staffs who worked in the capital city, the courts and administrative bodies located in town because it was the county seat, and the fact that it was by far the largest metropolitan area within a 5 hour pre-Interstate drive, and the Charleston of this era was anything but sleepy.

For a young Jewish lawyer, however, Charleston was a great dilemma. It was a place where opportunities were limited. The large and established firms simply did not have a position for Jews, women, or people of color. This was not unusual at the time throughout most of the United States. It is why the plaintiff's and criminal defense bars (lawyers representing the injured and those charged with blue collar crimes) were for so many years comprised heavily of minorities – they had no other choice.

This covert bigotry allowed State Bar Associations to adopt a shamefully over-reaching body of rules called the Canons of Ethics. These Bar Associations were charged with governing the practice of *all* lawyers in the State, but, in reality, they were run by the big firms. Ostensibly, these rules were to apply to all lawyers equally, but their intended result was to make the practice of law as difficult as possible for small-firm lawyers, and, by extension, their clients. Though no longer minority based, these same types of rules, I'm sad to say, still exist today, and still are usually applied against the lawyers representing regular people, rather than against those who represent corporations and insurance companies.

This world of excitement and challenge is the one Stanley E. Preiser and other minorities faced when they hung their shingles in the 1950's. However, significant difference in how Stanley would refuse to accept the *status quo* set him apart from the others, and drives a great deal of his story.

In the 1940's and 50's, the leading plaintiff's lawyer in Charleston, and a community leader as well, was a Jewish man named Samuel Lopinsky. It was "understood" that young Jewish lawyers who came to the area to practice would, in so many words, pay homage to Sam, who would then refer them cases and "take care of them." As you can probably discern by now, this did not sit well with young Stanley, who decided to do something about it. But what to do? It would be hard to attract business as a Jew if Sam didn't help. True to form, in 1952 Stanley opened his own office in the Union Building on the river, all the while fine-tuning a novel idea should business prove to be slow. Unfortunately, with no help from Sam, it was, and Stanley launched his plan.

You may recall the TV show *Remington Steele*, an early 80's staple starring Pierce Brosnan (before he took over the role of James Bond) and Stephanie Zimbalist. Zimbalist was a private investigator who was attracting no business because she was a woman. Rather than join an existing large firm, she "invented" Remington Steele and named her investigative agency after him – an obvious man. One day, however, a dapper gentleman (Brosnan) appeared, claimed to be Steele, and that was the comedic core of the show for its five-year life time. But the cultural comment revolved around the firm's clients believing Steele was the boss, and treating him in a manner accorded by that status, while, in reality, Laura Holt (Zimbalist) made the final decisions and owned the agency.

One might conclude Stanley was ahead of his time when he instituted the same strategy 30 years before *Remington Steele*. Stanley searched out a down-on-his-luck, tall, handsome, Irish-Catholic lawyer named John Lane, who had recently been turning far too often to the bottle. The peripatetic Lane had never shown much talent as a lawyer, but he could charm the birds out of the trees. Thus, the firm of Lane and Preiser was born in 1954, and to the world the order of the names reflected the pecking order of the two lawyers, and maintained the illusion of Lane's authority. In truth, Stanley owned 100% of the business, funded it as necessary, and made all the decisions.

Stanley also would relate that in the 1950's he would try any genre of case that came along, and estimated he spent about 200 days a year in the court room. If one realizes there are approximately 240 working days each year, that was 83% of his time. There is no substitute for that type of experience, which is precisely why Stanley did it, and, as law is now practiced, there never will be such an opportunity again.

During this time, business picked up quickly, and Stanley paid John Lane a handsome salary that allowed him to move into a new subdivision in the hills of Charleston. All was on the right track.

ROUND SIX

Trial Lawyers and Bar Associations

Stanley was only 26 years old when he established Lane and Preiser. Primarily due to his rejection of the "Lopinsky system," he was already becoming a leader among the state's Plaintiff's lawyers. Sam Lopinsky never forgave Stanley, not only for bucking the system, but also for stepping in as *a* leader, soon to be *the* leader.

Fast forward: The law gods must have been enjoying themselves on the day of *my* first solo deposition in 1977. The lawyer on the other side turned out to be Sam Lopinsky, and the deposition was to take place at his office. It was a small car wreck case, and Sam, who still had a thriving practice, represented one small insurance company. He was at that deposition defending that company against my client.

Because we both went to the same synagogue, I had known and heard of Sam Lopinsky for as long as I could remember, and because he was so respected and at least 40 years my senior, I always addressed him as "Mr. Lopinsky." Before I left the office for the deposition, I asked Stanley whether I should continue that practice. Stanley immediately said no: I was now a lawyer. As such, I was Sam's equal, as I was to all lawyers, and I wasn't to be deferential. I should call everyone by their first name.

And that is exactly what I did upon showing up at Sam's office.

"Hello, Sam," I said. He gave me a startled, sour look that left no doubt he was perturbed at my effrontery. During the subsequent proceedings, Sam called me a few names and made it clear early in the session that he was going to do everything he could to unnerve me (he would not be the last who would unsuccessfully try to take out his frustrations with my father on me). I never really thought about it until now, but maybe I started this little tiff by using Sam's first name, or maybe Stanley knew what Sam's reaction would be when he advised me to do it and was making me his unknowing proxy. Either way, it had lasting effects.

The deposition finally began, and in the middle of my questions to Sam's client, we took a recess. I took a walk and Sam stayed in the deposition room to have a long discussion with his client. Usually, conversations between attorneys and clients are privileged and strictly confidential, but that privilege can be deemed lost if the lawyer and/or client discuss the covered matters with, or in front of, someone else.

When we resumed the deposition and I began questioning Sam's client again, it was obvious Sam had coached him on how to answer questions, and the client was tailoring his previous testimony to fit what he had been told. I asked the client outright what his lawyer had told him during the break. Sam instructed his client not to answer that question because he believed his private conversation with the client was protected by the attorney-client privilege. But Sam had made a critical error.

I pointed out to him that no private conversation with his client had occurred. The court reporter had never left the room and had been privy to everything Sam and his client discussed. The presence of the reporter destroyed any privilege, I maintained, and his client (not to mention the reporter if I chose to depose her) was obligated to disclose the details of their conversation.

Lopinsky was livid. He berated me, accusing me of pulling a cheap trick. He had never seen anyone do this in 40 years of practicing law! Well, I suppose there is a first time for everything. We took it to the judge, who agreed with me that Sam and his client had waived any privilege by talking in front of the court reporter. The judge also ordered that I be allowed to ask both the client and the court reporter about what was discussed during the deposition break. Sam was truly embarrassed, and while I don't know if he was ever again on speaking terms with Stanley, I do know he never again spoke to me.

As mentioned, the Plaintiff's lawyers of the day, who were charged with trying to win fair compensation for injured parties, faced many hurdles, all set up by the insurance industry and the railroads through their confederates in the state legislature and on the supreme court. A few examples: There was in place the doctrine of "Contributory Negligence," which disallowed any recovery at all if the plaintiff was responsible for his injury *in even the slightest degree.* Also, there were draconian and burdensome rules making it nigh impossible for plaintiff's counsel to use demonstrative evidence. It sounds unbelievable in this age, but it's true. There were limits on death clams of (hold on to your hats) $110,000, and that remained the case until after I graduated law school. That pathetic limit gave rise to the not-so-funny joke that railroads fitted trains with a reverse gear so that if a train hit and injured someone, the train could just back up and run them over because it was often cheaper to pay off the family of a dead person then to compensate them for their injuries while alive.

It was also disheartening that lawyers on the side of the people had never been especially respected. To the vast majority of the public they were unscrupulous "ambulance chasers" who would do anything for a dollar (just watch an old film or two). Dedicated rooms at law schools, scholarships honoring venerated attorneys, political influence, and the like, were mostly confined to the world of the white male majority in old, established law firms.

The first case Stanley handled that was covered by the newspapers illustrates the uphill climb for the injured in 1952. Lewis Stone, a watchmaker, sued the U.S. Government for negligence when a heavy iron window grate at the post office fell and crushed his hand. A child had pulled herself up to the counter, causing the grate, meant for use when the post office was closed, to fall. The presiding judge would not let the case go to the jury, who are the people that are supposed to decide factual issues in dispute. The judge instead held that the child's action was an independent intervening cause. In other words, according to the court, it did not matter whether the grate was secured correctly, nor did it matter whether the Government had negligently failed to secure it. What mattered was that the child pulled on the counter. The judge threw out the case. Today, the results would probably be different and more aligned with common sense. Today, a court would likely find that it was reasonably foreseeable that a child, as children do, might pull on a counter and thus the defendant has a duty to secure any heavy grates to protect the public from injury.

Stanley, along with a small group of like-minded, dedicated, and talented men nationwide knew changes had to be made. As early as 1946 some of the country's brightest and most progressive lawyers formed the National Association of Claimants Compensation Attorneys (NACCA), with the goal of improving both the recovery prospects for the injured individual, and the public image of the Plaintiff's attorney. This they would do in their early days solely through the pooling of resources to provide top level legal education. In later years they also formed political action committees to help pass legislation for the good of the people. As time passed, the intensive learning and its application translated into larger verdicts, a more equal playing field, and respect for attorneys doing this kind of work. Stanley began reading NACCA material in law school, and immediately upon passing the Bar began to attend their meetings. He was the only one from West Virginia at the time, and for many years thereafter.

It is difficult to overstate the importance of NACCA (later known as the American Trial Lawyers Association, or "ATLA," the Association of Trial Lawyers of America, still "ATLA," and the American Association for Justice, or "AAJ"). NACCA was invaluable in helping to mature the civil justice system in the United States, which is, without doubt, the fairest in the world. Stanley didn't have the money for hotels, but he recognized the importance of the new techniques and novel concepts being taught, so he drove to Chicago to attend his first meeting in 1953, and slept in his car.

It wasn't long before Stanley was known within the Association, and began teaching others. He traveled throughout the country as instructor, and sometimes student, with the greatest trial lawyers of their generation. Through the use of new techniques in demonstrative evidence, psychological principles of investigation, persuasion, witness examination, and evidence bolstered by science, verdict amounts did indeed begin to rise. Members of NACCA took all these new concepts home, and by the end of the 1950's, most of these leaders had become stellar Plaintiff's lawyers in their individual states.

Larger verdicts led to more frequent and more detailed newspaper coverage. More interesting presentations kept the juries (and judges) interested, and they began to talk about these lawyers who were so impressive. People began to seek out the individual attorneys because they were winners. So was born around the turn of the decade, the celebrity lawyer – the *trial* lawyer -shockingly almost always lawyers on the side of the people. And according to Stanley, "The trial lawyer became the elite of the Bar, and has remained so."

In June, 1959, after touring the country with teaching caravans and attending a dozen NACCA national meetings, Stanley organized and led a group of eleven forward thinking lawyers to found the West Virginia Trial Lawyers Association – WVTLA (now the West Virginia Association for Justice). They met in Charleston and signed the founding documents. Besides Stanley, they were W.H. Ballard of Welch, Robert Ellis of Huntington, Robert Goldenberg of Parkersburg, Chad Ketchum of Huntington, John Lane of Charleston, L.F. Poffenbarger of Charleston, James Pyles of New Martinsville, S. Robert Reiter of Wheeling, Warren "Red" Thornhill of Beckley, Michael Tomasky of Morgantown, and Edward Zagula of Weirton. Only Bob Goldenberg was alive at the time I finished this work, but he passed away in mid-August.

As with John Lane five years before, Stanley felt the first President and face of WVTLA should be an establishment type to help build credibility and, ultimately, membership. Thus, L.F. Poffenbarger, the bearer of an old and aristocratic name, was chosen to lead. Behind the scenes it would be Stanley who did the work, arranged the educational programs, and schmoozed the press in order to get the word out about this fledgling organization, but to the public L.F. was the man.

By 1961, the WVTLA annual seminar, chaired by Stanley then and for almost 20 years thereafter, had achieved the justifiable reputation of being the top such educational program in the

United States. The finest and best-known lawyers and lawyer celebrities (Melvin Belli, Howard Cosell, Alan Dershowitz, Herold Price Fahringer, Henry Rothblatt, Tom Lambert, Gerald Spence, Marvin Mitchelson, Arthur Miller, Racehorse Haines, Justice Tom Clark, and all the national officers of ATLA) made frequent appearances in Charleston. Attendees came from up to 20 states, and the seminars were so large they sometimes needed to be presented in the Civic Center auditorium.

WVTLA's mission was mostly to teach the state's plaintiff's lawyers how to do a better job for themselves and their clients. Photos serve to memorialize the giants of the legal scene who came to Charleston every year. In fact, one of Stanley's ideas to enhance the brotherhood of the Plaintiff's Bar was to invite only speakers from out of state (with the exception of West Virginia judges and law professors) so there would be no jealousy among the members of WVTLA over who was on the program.

This clever scenario worked well. With one notable exception, I believe every plaintiff's lawyer of note in West Virginia was active in WVTLA until I moved to Boca Raton in 1992 and followed my West Virginia connections a little less closely. Stanley, already living in Florida, was absent from WVTLA except for returning to lecture. His guiding hand was not there, and it showed. Subsequent leadership changed the seminar plan to save money, and used state attorneys as instructors. Without a unifying individual, for a number of years there was great division and jealousy within the organization. Fortunately, today, in great part due to its Executive Director Beth White, WVTLA (now WVAJ) is back on track as the vital group it should be.

I personally became President of WVTLA in the mid 1980's. Until I had my own children, I did not understand the pride my father must have felt seeing his son become the head of a group he founded. By that time, due mostly to Stanley's efforts, WVTLA had solidified its reputation as the leading legal educational force in West Virginia, and was renowned for offering the best annual seminars, featuring the most coveted speakers, in the country. It had also become - and I do not say this lightly - the protector of the citizens' rights to open courts and just verdicts. That meant taking sophisticated actions designed to educate the public about those rights, and legislatively fighting the insurance and medical industries' lobbying for arbitrary limits on damages and selective exemptions from legal responsibility.

By 1960-61, Stanley had become well known and highly respected within NACCA. While some of the following names may no longer be on the radar of the trial lawyer community, they were the forefathers of the modern plaintiff's practice. The adequate awards for the injured and the rise in standing of the plaintiff's lawyer can be attributed directly to these pioneers, and they deserve mention here, not only for those reasons, but also because they were my father's friends whom I was privileged to know:

Mel Belli, Lou Ashe, and Bob Cartwright of San Francisco; Ted Koskoff of Connecticut; Tom Lambert of Boston; Craig Spangenberg of Cleveland; Bob Begam and Sam Langerman of Phoenix; Roscoe Hogan of Birmingham; Phil Corboy of Chicago; Jacob Fuchsberg, Harry Gair; Moe Levine, Al Julien, Al Averbach, and Joe Kelner of New York; George Allen of Richmond; Bill Colson and Perry Nichols of Miami; Benjamin Marcus and Harry Philo of Detroit; Ed Rood of Tampa; Alva Brumfield of Louisiana; J.D. Lee of Tennessee; David Shrager of Philadelphia; Leon Wolfstone of the state of Washington; Orville Richardson of Missouri; and James Dooley of Illinois.

These men pledged their time and effort to educate plaintiff's lawyers nationwide, and in 1960 or 1961, Stanley joined 13 of them who traveled the nation on their own money doing just that. They were known as "Ed Rood's Rangers." They were legendary in their day, and formed the core of the national association. Naturally, NACCA needed a President each year, and among all these "chiefs" it was a hotly contested position. Stanley was asked to run many times over his career but he declined. That did not, however, stop him from wielding a great deal of influence behind the scenes, starting in 1962, as you will soon see.

Stanley's own involvement with NACCA/ATLA would stay strong for a quarter of a century. He sat on the Board of Directors for about that length of time; he served as Editor of the Association's magazine; he oversaw the Education Department as it expanded to running 20 programs a year; he chaired the Criminal Law section for a number of years; he appeared more than once before Congressional committees as ATLA's representative on the issue of the time; he was instrumental in helping establish the Women's Caucus; and he became one of the most popular speakers in the nation.

Until he retired, Stanley always made time to help the national leadership in any way he could. He often said, when declining an offer to run for office: "There is nothing so ex as an ex." By 1970, numerous West Virginia attorneys were attending the national seminars, where the speeches given by Stanley, a great orator, were almost always standing room only. On the state level, besides running the star-studded educational seminars, he also agreed to serve two terms as President.

The Trial Lawyers legacy of Stanley Preiser is celebrated and remembered in many ways. He was posthumously elected to the AAJ Hall of Fame. At the offices of the West Virginia Association for Justice, the conference room bears his name, as does the annual award for their outstanding member. As to the AAJ recognition, which that group only awards after death, I know Stanley always opposed that policy. He thought the honored lawyers would like to know. I am quite sure he would have liked to express his personal appreciation for the recognition.

Stanley was truly the soul of the West Virginia Trial Lawyers for their first 30 years. He served as President in 1962 and again in 1973, and had his hand, heart, and mind in every aspect of the organization. WVTLA could not have survived without him, and, though it probably goes without saying, his life would not have been the same without WVTLA.

ROUND SEVEN

Training at the Firm

It is understandable that people assume, even without knowing much else about him or her, that a lawyer with *many* years of experience is someone in whom they can put their trust. The flip side of that coin is the assumption that an attorney only out of school for a *few* years isn't ready to handle serious matters. While both of these beliefs might occasionally be correct, they are just as often unfounded.

The Bar is populated by many attorneys who have been practicing for decades, yet are still making the same mistakes they made 20 years before when they first graduated from law school. Perhaps they failed to attend quality and relevant continuing legal education and are out of date. Perhaps they never associated with attorneys of skill, and so never had the opportunity to learn through example. Of course, lawyers are required to attend a minimum number of hours of Continuing Legal Education (CLE) per year in order to keep their license, and compliance sometimes actually benefits attorneys. However, these educational requirements also are in great part designed simply to make money for the State Bar Associations. How so?

Bar Associations govern almost all attorney conduct. This includes setting required hours for CLE. What is rarely discussed is that because the law does not have formal specializations as one finds in medicine (Obstetrics, Cardiology, Pulmonology, or Neurology, for example), a lawyer can take his or her CLE classes in any field, no matter that s/he never handles matters related to the subject matter being taught. Because of this, many attorneys sadly choose to obtain their required hours at the most attractive vacation spot where one can sign in at 9:00 a.m., and then spend the rest of the day on a boat, for example. As long as the CLE program is recognized as legitimate, any lawyer can obtain their hours by attending. The Bar Associations do not care, or at least they don't have rules against this, despite their obligations to protect the public from unknowledgeable and/or inadequately trained lawyers. Naturally, lawyers should be permitted to learn new things and take classes in a novel area of the law. However, allowing lawyers to entirely forego any training in their usual areas of practice only benefits the educational organizations' bottom line, in which the Bar Associations are heavily invested.

Fortunately, there are lawyers dedicated to their particular craft, as well as organizations, as discussed above, that present programs designed to further the lawyers' knowledge and expertise. There are even groups that offer certification in some fields, meaning they recognize that some attorneys have met minimum standard for practice in certain areas of law.

In the trial field, lawyers willing to spend the time and energy to pursue such certifications usually rise to the top. Throughout the 1950's Stanley attended the finest trial seminars sponsored by NACCA at least twice a year, and brought what he learned back to his own firm, which continued to grow throughout the decade.

Stanley's devotion to continuing education, both for himself and the lawyers in his firm, resulted in Lane and Preiser attorneys establishing reputations as fearless advocates who were ultra-prepared, unafraid of the courtroom, and progressive in offering new ways to present evidence. Combine Stanley's constantly expanding knowledge base, his dedication to preparation, his flamboyant style, his photographic memory, and his crackling cross examinations, and he was winning case after case. Both the legal community and the public took notice.

It did not matter that the lawyers at Lane and Preiser had no previous extensive experience in the trial arena. What they learned at seminars and from Stanley put them squarely on a par with, or even above, most advocates in West Virginia, and increasingly nationwide. This was so throughout the time the Preiser name was attached to the firm. Attorneys were always encouraged to attend the major trial seminars at the firm's expense, and those that took these programs seriously were almost all universally successful, no matter where they chose to practice over the next 60 years.

Stanley was a hard taskmaster who wanted to waste no time in getting ahead professionally, and that included the desire to earn a living commensurate to the major corporation lawyers. It must be remembered that fair, substantially-sized verdicts in personal injury cases were not the norm until well into the 1960's. Up to then, a plaintiff's lawyer who was paid only if s/he won a case was essentially in a volume business, meaning s/he would need to win a large number of smaller cases if s/he was to make rent, support a growing staff, and take home substantive income.

In these early years, Stanley's firm followed a routine designed to achieve these goals. Few would believe the details in later years, but those that lived it know it to be true, and it established Stanley as the hardest working lawyer anyone knew. This reputation lasted well into the 1980's when he sold his firm, moved to Florida, and began to consult with law firms more than actively try cases.

When Lane and Preiser was formed in 1954, things took off.

Lawyers and staff were added at a rapid pace. In 1955, Stanley and Joyce had a second child, a daughter Terri, and purchased a new home in the Fort Hill section of Charleston, one of the nicest areas of the time. Expenses were up – keeping a house and raising two children isn't cheap, and Joyce understood that Stanley would have to put in extra hours. She would accept that over the years, and was always supportive.

Monday nights were designated as office meeting nights for all lawyers and investigators. They would discuss and evaluate every case, bring in food, and be expected to stay until the wee hours of the morning – no one left before 2:30 a.m. This tradition at the firm, interestingly, continued into the 1970s when so many cases were being handled that the firm employed four full time field investigators. At the end of these marathons, Stanley and the unmarried lawyers would go for burgers and hash browns at the Toddle House, the only all-night diner near downtown.

These Monday sessions enabled professional progress and built camaraderie. In the mid 1960's, Dad would allow me to sit in to listen and learn, and then evaluate the cases along with everyone else. Mom was none too happy about my hours spent in the office or the early-morning Toddle House milkshakes, but as long as my schoolwork didn't suffer, she put up with it. And I think Dad was always pleased I was interested.

On weekends, one lawyer was assigned to each of the record rooms in Charleston and in Logan. These county offices were officially closed, but Stanley, who prized his relationship with administrative personnel, had arranged to borrow keys from the clerks of both counties. The lawyers rotated and were able to earn good money for the firm by doing title searches from 9:00 to 5:00 in an otherwise closed office for 2 days every weekend. There certainly was nothing wrong with this arrangement, but I suppose Stanley was one of the few who ever thought to ask.

For those lawyers not doing record room duty, Saturday was considered a work day from 9:00 to 3:00 in the winter and 9:00 to 1:00 in the summer. Sundays were 1:00 to 4:00 in the winter, and a day off in the summer, though it was unusual not to find at least one lawyer/investigator/secretary team working to get ready for a trial the next day.

The balance of the week pretty well mirrored most busy, successful firms. Client meetings, some depositions, case investigation, settlement meetings, prep sessions, and trials filled the days and nights. Trials were more common then as most could be concluded in under two days. This was all in the time before CLE was required or even readily available, so Stanley's time was also spent taking on the responsibilities and burden of travel, absorbing lessons, and returning to share any newfound ammunition with his colleagues. He never seemed to mind.

Though he did not join Stanley until 1978, my close friend and attorney Ted Kanner, a former President of the West Virginia Trial Lawyers Association, captured the experience of every lawyer who would work with Stanley for the first time in his remembrance address about Stanley to the county Bar Association in 2010. In his words:

> *There was never a time in my life that I did not know Stanley Preiser. Inasmuch as I was born into the extended family of B'nai Jacob Synagogue, which he and his family attended, I always heard Stanley's name mentioned in the most revered tones. He was the preeminent trial lawyer in the community and state, and had a well-deserved national reputation. Anyone who aspired to the practice of law further aspired to work with and learn from the best, and I was privileged to do this by having joined Preiser*

& Wilson right out of law school in 1978, and working there until 1985.

In managing a lawsuit, Stanley not only always saw the big picture, he kept his eye on every detail with extensive use of check lists, memoranda, calendar systems, and to-do sheets. His legendary obsession with outworking the other side, preparation, and sticking to details drove his associates and partners crazy, but ultimately acted to serve his clients well, and made anyone who worked with him a much better lawyer because of the experience.

I remember the first major case on which I worked with Stanley in the late 70's. It was a fraud case against Massey Coal Company in which middle and upper management were (allegedly) shaking down contract miners for kick-backs and bribes. As we prepared for three days of depositions of witnesses, I worked countless hours reviewing contracts, statements, financial records, and other documents. Finally, as per our calendar and to-do list, I met with Stanley on the weekend before the depositions thinking I knew every detail of the case, and everything that could possibly be gleaned from a review of the documents. Boy, was I wrong.

That is when I was subjected to my first cross examination by Stanley. Although he had only spent a cursory amount of time with the file at that point, he showed me how little I knew about the case, how little I understood about what was pertinent, what little grasp I had of the legal nuances of the matter, and just how, well, how little I was in the presence of Stanley.

Although I didn't get much sleep that weekend, and even threw up a few times, I was prepared by the time we went to Beckley to take the depositions. Some were taken by Stanley, which were masterful, others were taken by me, which, at the time and in his presence, seemed pitiful. But ultimately my efforts weren't bad, and although I left several feet of stomach lining behind, the fact is that Stanley's preparation was incredible. Even to this day, I share with many lawyers who worked with Stanley the thought that when confronting a legal, business, or even personal issue, I ask what would Stanley have done?

Gregg Rosen, an outstanding lawyer in Pittsburgh who worked with Stanley on many cases, answered Ted's question as it once involved Gregg:

Stanley and I began discussions in the very beginning of a defense of my client Bill Fiore, who was accused of ordering the hit of the head of the Bureau of Solid Waste Management for the Pennsylvania Department of Environmental Protection. The trial was scheduled for Greensburg, Pennsylvania, a more rural area about 50 minutes east of Pittsburgh. Stanley immediately said that we would visit the Goodwill store, purchase some old ill-fitting clothing, and then spend three or four days sleeping in a fleabag Greensburg hotel and eating in rundown diners so that we could get to know the potential jury pool and its "weltan-schauung" - my word, not his, meaning a particular outlook on life. Stanley had a very good vocabulary, but he rarely flouted it while speaking. I suspect it was the result of years training himself to speak to jurors in language they could understand. William F. Buckley, Jr. was never in the jury pool.

By the end of the 1950's, Lane and Preiser was one of the pre-eminent plaintiffs' firms in the state, and Stanley, himself, was personally and professionally ready to emerge as a leader on a number of fronts.

ROUND EIGHT

A Giant Emerges

By 1960, it had pretty well become an open secret as to who ran the firm of Lane and Preiser. Over the preceding six years or so there had just been too many people – firm members, secretaries, experts, referring lawyers, etc. – who had spent enough time at the office to be able to discern what was what. Further, John Lane had slowed down and was really not involved in the litigation side of things. He was most visible at Stanley's side, though still able to command attention with his regal looks and charming persona.

After L.F. Poffenbarger's term as the first President of WVTLA, John Lane was elevated to the position in 1961. Stanley would maintain this "secret partnership" for only another two years, while continuing to embellish John's legal acumen for the public and legal community to see. He would soon take this embellishment to the next level.

The year was 1962. The place was Seattle. A lawyer named Jacob Fuchsberg was running for President of NACCA. For some reason lost in the dust of history, Stanley was adamantly opposed to his election. Jack, as he was called and as the story goes, was from New York City and didn't much care about the opinions of some young West Virginia lawyer. I'm told that Jack was condescending and rude to Dad during this time, something that in later years people realized was not necessarily a smart move. Jack, too, soon learned that it was also folly to underestimate Stanley Preiser.

John Lane had just finished his term as head of WVTLA, and Stanley decided Lane should run against Fuchsberg for the NCAA Presidency. Never mind that John had not been active on the national level, knew almost no one, and had little idea as to how NACCA operated. Stanley had his back, he had a plan, and he got to work.

He threw a series of major parties for the membership to meet John. They drank a lot of Scotch and enjoyed fresh Washington salmon. John quickly rose from an unknown underdog to a serious challenger. Campaign parties like this are commonplace today, but this was an Association first. While there had indeed been some mild electioneering in the past, even that, Fuchsberg felt, wasn't necessary to defeat John Lane (whoever *he* was).

Of course, John J. Lane of Charleston, WV, who few in NACCA (soon to be ATLA) now recall, became its President. Unsurprisingly, Stanley spent a great deal of time that year at NACCA's home office in Boston calling the shots.

Jack Fuchsberg, meanwhile, had realized the error of his ways. He knew a good party when he saw one. In 1963 he asked Stanley to run *his* NACCA Presidential campaign. Stanley accepted. Fuchsberg won the election and later became a judge on the New York Court of Appeals. In the end, he and Stanley enjoyed a good, friendly relationship spanning three decades.

The following year Warren Thornhill of Beckley would become the President of the West Virginia Trial Lawyers Association. Thirteen years later I would become engaged to Warren's niece, Sara Thornhill, at an ATLA meeting in Monte Carlo. We would marry six months after that and Sara would, over the years, spend her own significant time at ATLA and WVTLA seminars and conventions, rising to the Presidency of the national Auxiliary. She and I are still lovingly married 42 years later. Back to Stanley.

ROUND NINE

1960's Private Life

Though he probably worked more than 90 hours per week, Stanley did all that he could to be an exemplary father and husband. When I was 7-14 years old, I remember my family having dinner together 4-5 times a week. Joyce would later point out that my memory on this was foggy. In reality, she said, we were lucky if Stanley was home for dinner twice in seven days.

Once I turned 15, I assume the number of family dinners decreased because of me and *my* schedule. I was heavily involved in sports, editing the school yearbook, finding dates, and had an after-school job at a pawn shop because Dad decided I needed to learn the value of a dollar. There were also youth groups, parties, friends, etc. If Dad was too busy to have dinner with the family, I didn't notice, which I suppose may impact my recollection of those days. Of course, what teen-age boy is concerned about his father's work schedule?

But I believe my misperception of the *quantity* of time Dad spent with us speaks to the high *quality* of the times we did have. I fondly remember dinners at home where my sister and I could each earn a dime (later a quarter) if we learned a new word from the dictionary that day. And the four of us often played games such as *Password, Match Game,* and a favorite that consumed lots of time on car trips as well, *Three Thirds of a Ghost*, a spelling exercise. Dad also met us downtown for Chinese food every Monday, and from there I would go to piano lessons when younger, and to the late-night office sessions when older.

Stanley also knew how to make father/son time especially memorable. For example, I had fallen in love with sports watching TV as Pittsburgh's Bill Mazeroski hit the walk-off World Series home run against the Yankees in 1960. I became a huge Pirates fan, and the next year Dad took me, then 9 years old, on a boys-only trip to Pittsburgh to take in a double header between the Pirates and the St. Louis Cardinals. Through the Pirates' lawyer, he arranged for me to sit in the clubhouse between games. I still have the autographs I collected that day from Roberto Clemente, Dick Groat, Elroy Face, Mazeroski, and, because he happened to be in the hall when I was leaving, "Stan the Man" himself – the great Stan Musial. I had heard people refer to my father as "Stan the Man" for many years. I didn't know until that day that there were two.

When I was a little older, about 12-15, Dad and Circuit (later Federal) Judge Dennis Knapp, would take Dennis' son and me once a year to Morgantown to see the West Virginia Mountaineers play football. Dinner was at Pizzeria Italia, which I thought served the best pizza in the world then, and continued to think so through law school in Morgantown seven years later. I even ended up representing the owner in a couple of matters after I started practice. College football and pizza. What more could a Dad give a son?

Back home, Dad, who no longer had much time for sports himself, bought books about basketball and tennis, and spent hours with me until I understood both games and could navigate the fundamentals. As you have read above, he was a great football player only 15-20 years before and still knew the game. He taught me to throw a spiral with the tip of the football up so it was easier for the receivers to catch, how to tackle with my shoulders and then roll the runner down in a way to protect myself, and how to rush a punter with arms crossed across my face so the ball wouldn't injure me if I got close enough for a block. He bought a ping pong table and spent time rallying with me. And he took a professional pool table as a fee and taught me angles and putting english on the cue ball. Though I only played sandlot football until organized fraternity intramurals in college, I became a ranked tennis player, a tournament table tennis competitor, a fair pool player, and the leading scorer on some pretty good basketball teams. Dad hardly ever missed a game. A lot of credit for my sports success goes to him.

Stanley also taught me to fight, harkening back to his boxing and street experiences. There were a couple of bullies in the neighborhood who were older and bigger than I, and Joyce pressured Stanley to talk to their parents about leaving me alone. Dad disagreed, feeling I had to learn to take care of myself. I ended up fighting them both at different times – pretty quick fights, actually, as one block, one feint, and a sock to the face sent them home crying. It was then *their* parents, ironically, who ended up seeking Dad out to complain about my tactics. Not surprisingly, they got nowhere with him, and I can't recall being picked on again. Well, at least until Sam Lopinsky came along.

There were other social functions and events Stanley attended as a devoted husband and father. He had promised to buy my sister Terri a horse when she turned 6 years old, mostly to get her off his back when she was 4 and pining for a pony. But she remembered, he came through, and Stanley spent a great deal of time making sure she was trained to ride, and the horse was trained for the ring. He also spent time attending horse shows where Terri rode her reputed nag of a horse to a number of local and regional championships (more about horses later).

Of course, Joyce was never left out. Stanley escorted her to dinners and parties on Friday and/or Saturday nights, and asked her to travel with him to week long conventions twice a year. There, he would work during most days, but he and Joyce would also live it up on fishing boats, at receptions, at dinners, sightseeing, or simply relaxing at the pool with umbrella drinks or Martinis. Their best home movies have them in Las Vegas more than once hanging out at about 5:00 a.m. with Dean Martin and other night-owl entertainers. Though Stanley would probably have preferred to be at the dice table, Joyce was a celebrity groupie, and Stanley always tried to do what he could to make her happy.

As for politics, somehow, and for some reason Stanley had registered as a Republican. This was very strange in pre-Trump era West Virginia, especially in 1948 during the Truman candidacy. Perhaps he was looking ahead, as he was in favor of Eisenhauer over Stevenson in both 1950's campaigns, but after that (except for the McGovern candidacy and Carter's run for re-election) he always voted Democratic on the national level. In fact, he was involved in the Jack Kennedy campaign, though you will read later how he despised Robert. As for Trump, Stanley knew him in the 70's and disliked him intensely for what Stanley felt was his dishonesty and laziness. Discussing issues with Trump was a waste of time, Stanley always felt, because Trump was so uneducated in so many areas and never made an effort to learn. Stanley also thought Trump an extremely rude individual, but was willing to concede he probably didn't know any better.

When home, much of my parents' social life in the 60's was spent at the Southmoor Country Club, then located on a not-very-desirable tract of property on a hillside in South Charleston. Until the middle to late 1970's, Jews were not permitted to join the big time, plush country clubs. This was so not only in Charleston but in most places in the south. So more often than not the Jewish communities established their own. It gives one something to think about that even into the fourth quarter of the twentieth century, most of the "greatest generation" still stuck to their own when it came to social events — sometimes because they had no choice.

Difficult as it was for the Jews, African-Americans experienced bigotry in much worse forms, and on an open level well into the 80's, when it became less fashionable to be a segregationist. Yet it still existed then, as it does today.

The most glaring example of the Charleston community's racism of the times occurred in 1959, when the Minneapolis Lakers came to play an NBA game in Charleston. They featured Rod Hundley, a local boy who had gone on to All-American fame at West Virginia University, and Elgin Baylor, the best rookie in the league out of Seattle University. Baylor, along with two other teammates, happened to be Black.

When the Lakers stepped into the old Kanawha Hotel, one of the city's best, they were told the hotel is a "respectable place" and the "colored players" can't stay there. The team left as a whole and stayed in a predominantly Black establishment in the back side of town called Edna's Tourist Hotel. That only solved half the problem, as Charleston restaurants would not feed the three men of color. Well, Baylor refused to play the next day and was raked over the coals by the Charleston business community. Mayor John Copenhaver made it clear that in his opinion, "The city of Charleston has done nothing wrong."

Though Stanley was very close to many of his Gentile colleagues (especially in the Trial Lawyers' Associations), I never knew my parents to socialize with the non-Jewish community except at legal or other business-related meetings. However, he did have one particular friend that we visited every Christmas day beginning when I was in grade school, and for many years after.

The friend's name was William Dandy, a Lebanese or Syrian (he never committed) Christian. He, his wife Naz, and daughters Debbie, Karen, and Lisa, were like our family. Willie prepared delicious dishes we didn't eat at home – fresh ham, oyster dressing, and Syrian bread. Chess, checkers, and other games were played by all. And what was probably the favorite moment for both families each year was when we placed the Star of David at the top of the Christmas tree, which is something the Preiser household did not have. If the eight days of Chanukah spanned over Christmas, we would bring a Menorah and light the candles together. Dad truly looked forward to it. Upon reflection, spending a full day only once a year with a non-Jewish family seems odd today, but at the time I never thought much about it.

The Southmoor club, a weekly poker game, and some rollicking parties mostly took care of Stanley and Joyce's social wants and needs. I often prepped the chips for Murray (Sandy) and Sanford (Zel) Lewis, Alan (Sevy) Masinter, Stan (Judy) and Sam (Sugar) Rubin, Paul (Marcia) Friedberg, and my Dad when the game was at our house. Their party crowd included the above (wives in parentheses) along with David and Gloria Bass, Bob and Thelma Levine, Sherwin and Lanie Steiger, Eddie and Noonie Stabins, Bob and Dottie Garner, Frank and Marion Baer, and Alvin and Gayle Preiser. I was the coat boy when the group was at our house during cold weather.

The Club offered a swimming pool, a clubhouse, tennis courts, restaurant, and a sad nine-hole golf course with some fairways at slopes of 30 degrees or so. It could be a challenge. My parents played a great deal of golf, the one sport Stanley enjoyed with some regularity throughout his life. Naturally, he wouldn't compete until he was on a par, so to speak, with the best. He won Club Championships in Charleston, and later in Florida, though a few of his Boca Raton friends jokingly complained about his high handicap.

For those who chose to pay dues, the country club was the center of Jewish social life until the early 1970's, when the county school board commandeered it to build a new high school. No matter that there were many places that would have served them better, or at least just as well. The school board would rather evict the Jewish community than others, despite an all-star array of lawyers, including Stanley, who challenged the taking of the property. In the end, the courts held that the school board, regardless of how unsavory its reasons, had the right to choose that location, and Southmoor Country Club faded into history.

About four years later, the private clubs opened up to the Jewish community, and, surprisingly to many of their long-time members, the sky did not fall.

ROUND TEN

1960 – October, 1975: Professional Life

It would be impractical to chronicle every case Stanley handled over the following 35 years. Yet there are quite a few that are worthy of inclusion because they were followed by a great many people, because they set standards or records, because they provide humorous anecdotes, or just because they are interesting. Much of the information from the 70's onward will come directly from the lawyers who worked with Stanley on a given case. Prepare for a wild ride through the legal world of Stanley Preiser.

Stanley handled three cases of state-wide interest in 1962. The first involved Mary Dunbar who had been a passenger in a truck driven by an employee of Gate City Transportation of Detroit. The truck driver hit another car, knocking Mary unconscious, and putting her in a coma for a period of time. She recovered with minor deficits. The case settled for nearly $120,000 – a figure that might seem like peanuts today, but it translates into about $1,000,000 in 2020 dollars. This kind of mammoth recovery was almost unheard of back then.

The next case of interest was tried in federal court in Clarksburg, West Virginia. Robert Maxwell, who would one day become a United

States District Judge for the Northern District of West Virginia, was the U. S. Attorney in a case against G.T. Aluminum Company executives who had been indicted for mail fraud. After Maxwell called some 34 witnesses against the defendants, the sitting judge, Harry Watkins, threw the case out of court. Stanley, after vigorously cross examining most of the Government's witnesses, and without calling any witnesses for his clients, had convinced the judge that the charges were so minor they did not belong in federal court in the first place. I have found no record of the two defendants being prosecuted again.

The third case was another high-profile federal criminal trial, which took place in December, 1962, in Charleston. Stanley represented two men charged with stealing 680,000 pounds of steel from the former Naval Ordinance plant in South Charleston with intent to defraud the Government. As occurred in Clarksburg, the sitting Judge, John Field, dismissed the case after the conclusion of the Government's presentation of the evidence and Stanley's cross examination of the witnesses. The judge held that the Government had failed to meet its burden of proof, and that there was no way the evidence offered could support a guilty verdict that was "beyond a reasonable doubt." Stanley was again not even called to put on his client's defense.

Stanley was on a roll.

By mid-1963 it was time for Stanley to end the fiction that he was the junior lawyer in the firm. In fact, the way Stanley told it, some of the Circuit Judges helped him come to this conclusion. The story, confirmed to me by some of these judges, was that by 1963 Stanley had tried dozens of cases before all of them. He always informed the jury on summation that he was a young lawyer, and humbly asked them not to hold any mistakes he might have made against his client. At some point, the judges had simply had enough of Stanley calling himself a young lawyer and suggested it was time to give it a rest. Stanley took the "advice" to heart, and decided the firm's name should also reflect the truth.

At about this same time, John Lane was exhibiting health and other problems. He was ready to retire from the law and move to California, where, sadly, he passed away before the decade was out. John's retirement put an end to Lane and Preiser, and by late 1963, the firm of Preiser, (Bill) Weaver, and (George) Daugherty had been born, and quickly began to expand.

Stanley's most notable case of 1963 involved our friend Willie Dandy, who hosted us on Christmas Day for so many years. The case frequently made front page news. It involved well known Charleston police officers, multiple defendants represented by many local lawyers, and a highly-visible defendant in Dandy. Willie was an esteemed Charleston businessman, and President of United Beverage Company. He was indicted on a charge of receipt of stolen property. Allegedly, he had received an entire semi-truck full of hot cigarettes and delivered them to co-defendant carnival owner Natie Brown, who had been one of the few professional boxers to go the distance with Joe Louis.

Brown later taught Stanley the "ins and outs" of the carnival business. I was lucky enough to be along for those lessons and learned why you can't beat the games on the midway.

Back to the trial. Stanley believed the wide-spread news coverage had tainted the impartiality of any local jury pool, so he set out on an epic battle to have the venue changed. He called almost every top Charleston lawyer and businessman to the stand to testify that Dandy could not receive a fair trial in Charleston. Finally, the case was moved 60 miles west to Huntington. There, Stanley ripped apart the testimony of the major prosecution witness, detective Robert Crouse. Once Stanley was finished, Crouse had lost all credibility, which led to Dandy and Brown's full acquittal in 1964.

A few years later, Crouse began having disputes with the city administration. I happened to be home for either a long college Christmas break or a quick summer one, and I remember Bob Crouse, who had hated Stanley since his witness stand debacle, surprisingly making an appointment to see my Dad in his office. I was there when Bob said, "Stanley, I will never forgive you for what you did to me on the stand, but my career is in jeopardy and I need a good lawyer. You are the best I ever saw. Will you represent me?" Stanley took on the case in 1969, and Bob was reinstated to the force from which he had been suspended. More serious charges came about in January of 1972, which resulted in Bob's total dismissal from the police force. After these hearings, the Police Civil Service Commission fully reinstated and exonerated Bob, holding that the evidence the Mayor relied on to suspend had been insufficient. I don't know whether Bob ever actually forgave Stanley, but once Stanley became his personal lawyer, the two men enjoyed, if not a friendship, the benefits of a mutual, valuable acquaintanceship.

Returning to the 60's, in May of 1964 six men were arrested and charged with violating laws against working on Sundays. Commonly known as "Blue Laws," these statutes against doing business on Sunday existed in various forms nationwide. The defendants were owners, managers, and even one customer, of a leading discount chain and a local store. They needed to be open on Sunday to serve many customers who could not get away any other day, including those who observed the Sabbath on Saturday.

The defendants engaged Stanley as their attorney. He took the position that the "Blue Laws" violated the religious freedoms guaranteed by the United States Constitution. Proponents of the law, including Legislator William Brotherton, later a state Supreme Court Justice, maintained that people need Sunday to worship and should not work, putting the controversy squarely into a religious context. Accordingly, any lawyer challenging the "Blue Laws" would inevitably come under heavy scrutiny.

Stanley argued that any government establishment of only Sunday as a day of rest violated Constitutional protections requiring separation of church and state. He pointed out that many people indeed observed the Sabbath on Saturday, and thus needed to work and/or shop on Sunday.

The case would take up much of the year with the usual legal wrangling, procedural hurdles, etc. In Autumn, the Circuit Court denied the Defendants' Motions to Dismiss and ordered the parties to trial. Stanley filed a Writ of Prohibition asking the Supreme Court of West Virginia to block the trial, primarily on religious freedom grounds. Oral argument before the state Supreme Court commenced in January of 1965.

Later that year, the Supreme Court struck down the Statute, prohibited the trial of the Defendants, and ordered them released. That, as they say, was that, but the result added even more luster to Stanley's reputation.

In November of the same year, the case of *Edward Holstein vs. Chemical Van Lines* went to trial. Stanley was requesting the then-unheard-of sum of $350,000 (close to $2,200,000 in 2020 dollars) for Mr. Holstein, who had been injured when the truck in which he had been traveling collided with another vehicle. The plaintiff's claim was for reimbursement of medical bills, and compensation for reduced mental and earning capacities.

J. Campbell (Cam) Palmer was an arrogant, big-firm civil defense lawyer who showed open disdain toward both injured parties and their lawyers. I can remember his attitude as if the trial occurred yesterday. Stanley succeeded in persuading the jury to return with a verdict of precisely the $350,000 requested. It was the largest personal injury verdict in West Virginia history at the time. Defeating Palmer so soundly was a particularly pleasurable bonus.

By the latter part of 1965, Stanley had decided to sever his relationship with Bill Weaver and George Daugherty, and W. Dale Greene, a truly nice man and a good lawyer, became a partner in the firm of Preiser and Greene in 1966.

Despite Stanley's frequent involvement with the higher profile matters, he had not stopped trying what he referred to as his "bread and butter" cases. Mostly these were smaller damage cases (*very* small to most other attorneys of the time) involving soft tissue injuries undiagnosable by x-ray. It was Stanley, more than any other lawyer nationwide, who developed the techniques to successfully try this type case and obtain a fair verdict.

He became so well known for his expertise in this area that he lectured about it in over 35 states, built an unlikely following for such an unexciting area of the law, and ultimately, in 1966, wrote his first book, appropriately titled *Preparation and Trial of a Neck and Back Sprain Case*. It became a smash best seller among members of the Bar. After I became a lawyer in 1976, I rarely spoke to a plaintiff's trial attorney that did not bring up the book, and tell me how it had guided them to many successful results.

Almost anything in Stanley's book could be used for any injury case (and much of it for cases of all kinds). He included check lists, witness suggestions, investigation tips, advice on jury selection, and cross examination methods, for example. Many of the following techniques Stanley used 55 years ago to prove damages are either passé today, or outdated by new diagnostic aids, but they were novel at the time.

In soft tissue injury cases, it was commonplace in those days for the defense lawyer and his (there were no women) doctor to perpetuate a fraud on the jury by showing an x-ray of the part of the body the Plaintiff claimed was injured, and then telling the jury that since the x-ray demonstrated no problem, the Plaintiff was exaggerating, or even perhaps lying.

Stanley, in effect, put an end to this. During the Plaintiff's case, Stanley would take the x-ray, which is nothing more than a negative of a picture, and reverse it so it became a positive. The jury could then read it. Stanley would then have the Plaintiff's own physician use colored markers to draw in the ligaments, tendons, and whatever else was needed to show the tearing and stretching of those anatomical parts. Then the jury could understand that x-rays only showed the bone, and had nothing to do with the case. When the defense doctor then took the stand with his untruthful claim that the Plaintiff was not injured because the x-ray showed nothing, the jury already knew better, and Stanley would literally roast the defense doctor on cross examination for his lies. It wasn't long before that charade ended.

Stanley also made generous use of sophisticated medical illustrations and anatomical models to enable the jury to understand how the human body reacts to various forces. He was a pioneer in the use of biomechanical engineers to enhance and explain these forces from an engineering standpoint (the body being a machine, after all).

It was usually difficult to find any doctor who would say a soft tissue injury would be permanent. Of course, the longer the damage would last, the greater the verdict should be. Stanley developed a manner in which to elicit what was needed. Instead of asking whether the injury was permanent, he would ask, "Doctor, would you agree Mr. Smith will have pain and problems on and off for the rest of his life?" The treating physician almost always agreed, and more than just occasionally, when the question was put to them in that fashion, defense doctors would concede it was so.

In cases where the damage to the vehicle in which the Plaintiff was riding was slight, which allowed the defense to argue the Plaintiff was exaggerating a serious injury because s/he had barely been hit, Stanley used engineers to show how the energy of a wreck that may not have severely damaged the vehicle instead had traveled to the injured party. Energy has to go somewhere. Again, juries understood and awarded fair verdicts. Before this, lawyers would hardly have thought of using engineers because the cases were too small to pay for another expert. No longer.

Stanley taught early that there was a significant difference in lost earnings (which is what an injured party *actually* lost after a wreck) and lost earning capacity (what a working Plaintiff might lose in the future). The gray area here was when the Plaintiff was not a working person. Stanley helped pioneer the concept that even non-working people are entitled to compensation if they *no longer* could work if they wanted to.

Finally, Stanley recommended working with language and other communication specialists to develop better ways to connect the jury to the pain suffered in terms of both severity and length.

It was a combination of all the above that served to make the once so-called "little case" often worthwhile to try to its fullest.

With limited exceptions, attorneys are not permitted to advertise that they are "specialists" in a given area of the law. However, by the time Stanley published his book, attorneys were beginning, as had doctors years before, to specialize in narrower fields of practice. That trend has continued through the modern day, where even in the trial field some attorneys specialize in criminal work, some in injury cases, some in tax cases, some in product liability cases, some in professional negligence cases, some on domestic relations cases, etc.

Stanley was one of the last great generalists, so to speak. He always believed a good trial lawyer could try any kind of case, and, if handled correctly, an adequate verdict could be obtained in any venue. One can always learn about the subject matter that sets the parameters of each confrontation, be it medicine, tax, mechanical engineering, or any other field, but *all* trials are inherently about persuasion, and *that* discipline was the specialty of the trial bar in his mind. As he got a little older, and great generalists like Mel Belli of San Francisco, Theodore Koskoff of Connecticut, and Racehorse Haines of Texas, began to retire or pass away, Stanley may have become the last of the species. He could try almost any kind of case, and did.

By the time he was 40, Stanley had achieved that rare stature accorded the finest lawyers in the land.

Richard Hailey, one of the country's most respected and versatile lawyers, and the first African American President of the Association of Trial Lawyers of America, reflects on Stanley's influence on his life:

> *After law school at Indiana University and then receiving an LLM in International Law from Georgetown, I opened my practice in Indianapolis. It didn't take long before I thought my career to be stagnant and I began to look around to see if I might fit better in another state. I gradually became even more negative about the career opportunities for an African American professional in the conservative Midwest. I wanted to be where verdicts would be more in line with what I felt my clients deserved.*

By summer of 1985, I had become a regular at what was then called The American Trial Lawyers Association's (ATLA) Annual Summer Convention. Great lawyers abounded, but to me none stood out more than Stan Preiser – a man equipped with the mind of a nuclear physicist and the body of a middleweight boxing champion. He could not only practice law, but he could teach, and he believed that a real trial lawyer could try any type of case once he was armed with knowledge of the substance of the controversy.

During that convention, Stanley invited me to have drinks at the hotel bar. I confided that I was down on my experiences in Indiana, and sought his advice. I will never forget what happened next. Stanley looked me in my eyes and said, "Don't you ever complain again about the opportunities you've been given to be a great lawyer. You try your cases where you find them. Once you develop a standard of excellence, the results will follow." I was stunned at his directness and the sternness in his voice. He concluded, "Look at me. Look at me!! I'm a short Jewish lawyer from West Virginia and I've gone on to win cases in my home, small counties, and all over the United States." He then invited me to stop my bellyaching and rededicate myself to being the best lawyer I could be. Stanley was right. Success comes from within. Not three years later my wife, Mary Beth Ramey, and I obtained the highest collected medical malpractice verdict in the history of the state of Indiana. I am proud to say that it is a record that stands to this day. It was indeed not the venue — it was the lawyer himself that needed to recommit to excellence.

The second half of the 1960's, a time of continued success, rocketing fame, and a growing bank account, brought significant changes for Stanley, his firm, and his family. The outside trappings of Stanley's life had to keep up with his growing reputation as a lawyer and a leader. A relatively small and unimpressive home, a traditional office of this and bygone eras, and a simple stable for the horse (which by then had become horses), were no longer sufficient.

Most of the lawyers working for Stanley were West Virginia born and raised. At a time when Stanley was becoming more nationally prominent, he was seeking to add an urbane, top trial lawyer. He found the right person in Princeton graduate Donald R Wilson. Don had been publisher of a newspaper in Los Angeles, President of a college in Georgia, and National Commander of the American Legion. He was sophisticated, always perfectly dressed and coiffed, possessed a brilliant mind, and knew his way around the courtroom.

Having come to Clarksburg, West Virginia, to actually practice law, Stanley asked him to make another move, this time to Charleston. Don took the offer, and with his attractive younger wife Judy, made the transition. It was to be a superlative move all around for both him and Stanley.

My sister and I were enamored with summer camps, first in the Tennessee Appalachians, and then in the mountains of western North Carolina. Starting in 1962 we would be away for two months every summer giving our parents a pretty good rest. Terri would attend camp every summer until about 1966, while I kept going through the summer of 1969.

In August, 1966, we flew back to Charleston never expecting that instead of heading to our home of 11 years, we would be taken to a large, brand new house in the tony Louden Heights section of the City – a relatively flat area on the top of the southern hills. The home boasted a cascading staircase in the entrance foyer, a large master suite, a spacious kitchen and family room, "extra" bathrooms, and a beautifully landscaped swimming pool (not many private homes had pools in 1960's West Virginia). A newly slated and felted pool table in the finished recreation room downstairs ensured that this Williamsburg Way home was always busy – Stanley and Joyce entertained often at the pool and I, in high school starting that year, enjoyed hosting a slew of new friends, along with my old ones once they learned about the swimming pool and pool table.

The pool table was professional, having come from one of the local pool halls as a fee for one of Stanley's cases. Stanley's own teen-age years quickly returned, and for the first year he stalked the table like "Fast Eddie" in *The Hustler*. It was apparent he had spent a great deal of time with the stick in his youth (not really surprising for one who grew up during the war), and now he was enjoying playing again and teaching me. As usual, he did a good job with the latter. Many a weekend night the kids came over, we put a stack of 45's on the record player, and shot pool and drank beer into the early morning hours. It was hard to beat me. My classmates didn't spend much time at pool halls.

By 1968, the law firm had grown substantially. It was time to find new space. Fortunately, one of Stanley's clients, Fred Haddad, was experiencing tremendous growth and accompanied wealth as founder and CEO of Heck's, one of the pioneering super discount stores (much like a Walmart today). Fred was building a brand-new edifice on the river for his office, and Stanley leased a half floor for the firm, and contracted for himself use of the penthouse, with gym, sauna, kitchen, bedroom, and locker room.

The significance of this move was two-fold. First, it allowed the firm to design the lay-out as would best enable them to practice, and, two, the offices were decorated like no other law firm in West Virginia, and like few in the country. They resembled the homes of the gentry, with lush carpeting throughout, stylish wallpaper individually chosen by each attorney for his (still only men) office, custom made furniture, including plush leather chairs and fine wooden desks, and the most up to date equipment. The waiting room was a place of comfort and elegance, with a Chippendale sofa covered with black and white crewelwork imported from India surrounded by black leather wing chairs. The carpet was a specially woven red that would also grace Stanley's private office, and the white walls featured red Italian silk brocade wall hangings.

Yet the real show-place was Stanley's private office, finished in "manly" tones of cordovan and olive. A native stone fireplace was nestled between floor to ceiling bookcases, which, along with the wall paneling and ceiling beams, were constructed of solid oak. Two high back chairs upholstered in crushed velvet were prominent, and draperies, made in Switzerland, depicted a medieval castle scene, which was carried through to tables and wall decorations.

There were some other interesting touches that were far from common in those days. Stanley's double oak entry doors were held open by a magnet on the wall. He could throw a switch from his desk to close them. Draperies opened and closed by a second switch. Slide back a long panel door and you would find a full (and fully stocked) wet bar and a private bath with a telephone.

The *Charleston Gazette* was one of the two largest, and certainly the most powerful, newspaper in the state. To its publisher, Ned Chilton, that meant he was above the rules of decency. A few of his reporters served as Chilton's "hit men," and would print stories of people on a whim, rather than as a result of good reporting. And he had a cadre of senior staff that would also do his bidding, and who made up the Editorial Board. (This is not to say there were not some fine reporters on the staff from time to time – Andy, Paul, and others – you know who you are). But when false stories hit the press, Stanley was one of the few lawyers who would stand up and sue the *Gazette.* Chilton hated him for it, for he could not understand how anyone could challenge the right of the press to write what they wanted, regardless of truth.

Chilton would do all he could over the years to disparage Stanley. Some people (more than two) said that Chilton hated Stanley because Stanley had dated Chilton's wife when they were teenagers. This could be true. Chilton was a petty man. The feelings were mutual. Stanley intensely disliked Chilton, as well.

Knowing of this animosity, someone presented Stanley with a glazed ceramic tile bearing the *Gazette's* logo. He wasted no time installing the gift directly in the toilet bowl of his private office bath. It became one of Stanley's favorite *objets d'art.* He loved to show it off, and it became legendary among his associates and friends. One of the firm's lawyers with a devilish sense of humor sent a picture of the toilet and its enhancement to the *Gazette,* but I never saw Chilton run a story on it. Call it celebration or commemoration, when Ned died there were a few toasts made in the office that night.

Great lawyers have handled many cases about which the public hears nothing. Often there is a civil settlement the parties want kept quiet, but far more frequently, an impending indictment is halted before anyone really knows about it. Stanley was involved in a number of those types of defenses.

At the time when all the Watergate indictments were coming down, Stanley flew from Charleston to meet a public figure who was involved with the Administration. The targeted defendant was rightly worried about an indictment's effect on his reputation. He insisted, and the evidence seemed to confirm, that he was completely innocent. Stanley was able to stop the indictment, and the man was able to get on with a life that many admired.

But even with all his cases, Stanley stayed busy on the home front as well, and, to honor Don Wilson's contributions, in late 1973 or early 1974 the firm name became Preiser and Wilson.

In an ironic confluence of events, Stanley was representing Lashinsky Brothers Productions at the same time my sister Terri was becoming ever-more obsessed with horses. The Lashinskys were Charleston residents who had risen to prominence as promoters of concerts and other events on a nationwide basis. Sometime in the late 1960's they acquired the rights to the famed Royal Lipizzan Stallion extravaganza. At the same time, it was clear Terri envisioned a future in the equestrian field.

Naturally, Stanley would take a giant and creative step. In 1969, he built, and became the managing partner of, Colonial Stables in the Davis Creek section of Kanawha County. It offered about 20 indoor stalls, 30 outdoor stalls, indoor and outdoor riding rings, and equestrian lessons. As far as anyone knows, is was the largest indoor stables in the East – and when added to the outdoors stalls, it was huge. Stanley felt he had an ace in the hole. He thought my sister might do well running a horse-related business, but after a little while, it was apparent this was not, as it sat, going to be a lucrative enterprise.

So Stanley bought out his partners. Then, he and Gary Lashinsky reached an agreement whereby the Lipazzaner horses would be stabled and trained at Colonial. This was pretty exciting for all. It meant the influx of Europeans to train the horses and ultimately perform in the shows. It meant the pure white horses were born and raised at Colonial (they are black at birth). And it meant the stables would be bringing in some rent.

Ultimately in the mid 1970's, Lashinsky sold the show, so man and horse moved on. Terri was now running the place in name, but Stanley was spending an inordinate amount of time trying to keep it afloat. Then he had the brilliant idea to host indoor wintertime combination dressage competitions and rodeos every 6 weeks or so.

Even I, who am not really a horse lover, have to admit this was fun. Joyce and my wife Sara would run the concession counter (you can make a good profit on dogs and sodas), Stanley and I would roam the grounds making certain all was moving smoothly, and collecting money at various times from the entrance gates and the concession stand. Terri would be involved with the riders – both English and Western. While I never much cared for English dressage, the western events were thrilling. Barrel, Quarter horse, and pick-up races. I loved taking a break and sitting with the announcer, who was in a raised booth with an excellent sound system. He had this slow, mesmerizing drawl, and I can still hear him say with that West Virginia inflection, "Go lope those horses."

At the end of the evening, the family would pay out the prizes to the winners and the fees to the announcer and judge, and then sit and count the money. Stanley enjoyed having his whole family there, and while the total take would never match the lowest legal fee, there was something special and memorable about the experience.

One thing is for certain – just as Stanley was a great friend to so many people, he was a great father. Yet one has to evaluate everything in light of the era in which he and Joyce raised their children. The male was supposed to make grades, go to good schools, be well rounded, and ultimately be able to be independent and earn a good living. On the other hand, parents may have been pleased if females did the same, but it was not expected. They hoped their education would be adequate and that the daughter would find a husband with the traits of a man set out above.

Stanley tried to build a business for my sister at Colonial Stables because she loved horses. He also financed her trips to scores of horseshows, and by Terri's own count bought her eleven horses over the years. Stanley never made a nickel in the business, but he was satisfied that his daughter was happy – that's just how he was.

Alas, Colonial never made any real money and it closed down in the early 80's. Terri worked for other stables and ran at least one of her own, but I never knew any of them to be especially successful, nor do I know if Dad put any substantial funds into those businesses. He would invest in an entirely new endeavor with Terri, but I will get into that later.

John Romano, former President of the Florida Academy of Trial Lawyers and Southern Trial Lawyers Association, and who spent a great deal of time with Stanley during the last 10 years of his life, had this to say about Stanley and family:

> *Stanley was a human being I could talk about for days – as it has indeed been a rare privilege to actually know and spend quality time with a person who is a genuine legend as a court-room advocate. That observation though which touched me the most about this unique gift from God which we had in Stanley is that no matter where I was or what we were doing or what was happening....he always talked about his wife "Joyceeeeeeee," his children, and later – his grandchildren. I miss him so much.*

While doing research for this book, including searching the newspaper archives in four cities, I was genuinely shocked to discover not only the *number* of high-profile clients Stanley represented in the late 1960's and early 1970's, but also the breadth of subject matters touched by these cases.

His clients, at different times of course, included an Attorney General, a Banking Commissioner, a Commissioner of the State Road Department, the largest coal operator in Northern West Virginia, a number of prominent lawyers, an important union, white collar tax defendants, a major hotel, police officers, fire fighters, the Mayor of Lexington, Kentucky, and the State of West Virginia. He was handling appeals, criminal matters of all kinds (including a murder case), civil tax cases, corporate disputes, eminent domain controversies, and tort claims, mostly at this point medical negligence and product liability.

In one dispute Stanley represented some local hotel owners in a case opposite Holiday Inn, which was just becoming a megagiant. Stanley took a two-day deposition of Holiday Inn founder, Kemmons Wilson. It was reported to have been a grueling affair.

As fate would have it, not long after the Holiday Inn case resolved, Stanley, Joyce, and a couple from Vermont traveled early to the Bahamas or some other island for an ATLA meeting. Somehow there was a mix-up and no hotel had room for them for the two nights before the convention began. Stanley had a solution. They would go over to the Holiday Inn, tell the manager he was a good friend of Kemmons Wilson, and subtly cajole a room. This is what they did. The manager, a polite island native, asked to be excused for a second, went in the back, and a few minutes later out stepped Kemmons Wilson himself, who just happened to be in town. After Stanley deposed him a few months earlier, they were hardly friends, but Mr. Wilson was a gentleman, and found Stanley and the other three a room. You read correctly – Mr. Wilson gave all four of them one room with a King bed. The pictures of the Preisers of West Virginia and Lismans of Vermont under the covers together brought both couples (and others) huge laughs through the years.

The State of West Virginia had engaged Stanley to handle much of its eminent domain work, which involves a government entity's taking of private property for the public good upon paying a fair price. Primarily, land was being cleared to build the three Interstates and one major state Highway which would eventually converge in Charleston. These were pretty simple cases – each side had an appraiser who would give an estimate as to the value of the land, and the jury usually averaged the two and awarded that figure to the land-owner. Stanley was never quite satisfied with the average, however, and usually ended up doing much better for the State.

One day the Circuit Court had an error in the published trial schedule for eminent domain cases. Two judges had Stanley assigned to different court rooms at the same time, and for a number of cases. Incredibly, neither court would grant Stanley any relief, and both ordered him to be present at the same exact hour. The judges happened to share a secretary who had an office between the two courtrooms, so Stanley sat down in the secretary's office and simply refused to move until the judges worked it out between themselves.

They "magnanimously" gave him a three-hour postponement to find another lawyer in the firm to be present in one of their courtrooms. Alvin Hunt, who had experience with these type matters, was on vacation, but came to help Stanley out. But Alvin was not familiar with any of the particular cases being tried. So, in a scene that must have rivaled the funniest of farces, Alvin handled the direct examination of the State's expert in one courtroom while Stanley cross examined the landowner's expert in the other. They would then race thorough the common office, pass the baton as it were, and do the same thing again in the other courtroom. This went on all afternoon, and it allowed Stanley to handle all the cross examinations. Everything worked out well. When the two unreasonable jurists passed away many years later, Stanley closed the office each time, and had another party.

During the 1960's and early 1970's, the Jewish people of this country marched literally and figuratively with the African American community in its quest for the rights promised them by the Constitution. Jews and Blacks alike made up the famed freedom riders who traversed the south challenging the laws of segregation and facing violent crowds. Together, they also bore the brunt of severe physical attacks by racists like Birmingham's Commissioner of Public Safety, Bull Conner.

This was not an unsurprising alliance, as both groups understood and experienced bigotry in many forms, and American Jews have almost always supported the underdog. Stanley, having witnessed such prejudice first-hand through the years, had a deep attraction and commitment to the concept of justice for all. His firms always had a multitude of Black clients throughout West Virginia, and he always treated men in positions often filled by Blacks at the time, such as bellman, bootblacks, waiters, bus boys, and custodians, with kindness and dignity. The African American community, in return, respected Stanley and would do whatever they could to help him.

I asked Dad one time how he could so deeply relate to the Black community but was able to accept the segregation in seating, restaurants, water fountains, etc. when he had been a high school and college student in the Virginias. He thought a while and answered, "You know, it's just the way it was. We hardly thought about it. I have tried to make up for my silence ever since."

Around 1971, Stanley was asked to draft a new amendment to the West Virginia Human Rights Act. This Amendment would prohibit housing discrimination based on race, religion, color, national origin, and ancestry. He drafted the Bill and it was adopted by the West Virginia Legislature. Twenty years late, the law governing housing discrimination was separately enacted as the West Virginia Fair Housing Act.

In 1987, two courageous Charleston police officers, Harvey Bush and Casey James, organized all the African American police officers and firefighters to approach Stanley with a request that he file an affirmative action case on their behalf. There had not been a promotion to officer's rank in over 10 years within either group. Stanley suggested these outstanding and long tenured servants of the city engage me, and with the help and advice of my associate David Fryson, we succeeded in obtaining what we were told was the most sweeping consent decree guaranteeing the plaintiffs' rights in the country.

Stanley never charged a fee to any law enforcement officer or firefighter of any color, such was his respect for the work these men and women do for woeful wages. I'm proud to say my firms continued that practice.

I was incredibly moved and honored when not too long after the decree, Dallas Staples, a Black man, was elevated to Chief of Police and asked me to pin his bars on him during the swearing in ceremony.

Although we have a long way to go, in an era when many whites are rightfully re-examining our historical inactions and silence in the face of oppression against African American, Stanley was, and I am, proud that we and our firms had at least taken baby steps toward breaking that silence.

We here in the United States tend to refer to a block of three dangerous entities as an Axis of Evil (Germany, Italy, and Japan in World War II, and N. Korea, Iran, and Iraq according to George Bush, for example). Into the 1970's, big coal, the insurance industry, and railroads qualified as West Virginia's Axis of Evil. They opposed any progress toward fair compensation for the injured, or expansion of causes of action, and they were aided by their elected cohorts in the Legislature. Their influence made it very difficult to be a Plaintiff's attorney.

As the Plaintiffs' Bar improved, and its natural allies, the unions and consumer groups, became more powerful, there was finally enough money and influence available to convince quality candidates to run for all three branches of government and win. In this way, the "Allies" little by little broke through the Axis' obstruction to good through the 60's and 70's.

Briefly, a few words about the judicial branch. Since West Virginia became a state in 1863, its West Virginia Supreme Court of Appeals had been composed of Neanderthal-like men who were happy with the pro-big business slant of the laws. But with the election of Fred Caplan in 1962, the tide began to change. Justice Caplan was on the Bench until 1980, and some terrific men would join him. They included Jim Sprouse for two years before he went to the Court of Appeals; Charles Haden for three years before he joined Judge Sprouse; Don Wilson, who agreed only to serve out Chuck Haden's term, and in one year on the Court left an indelible mark of brilliance; and Richard Neely, the state's closest thing to a patrician. One might expect Justice Neely to have protected big business – but he was an outstanding and fair jurist for 22 years; Tom Miller, a truly cerebral former defense lawyer who highlighted balance and fairness for 16 years; and Tom McHugh, a "Miller-like" jurist who lawyers were happy to have judge their cases. Justice McHugh was the only one of the above who did not serve with Caplan.

Before 1977, West Virginia had never even had a million-dollar verdict in a personal injury case. The talented gentlemen listed above not only brought West Virginia law out of the dark ages, but elevated it to a level where it was the envy of fair-minded people nationwide. One could now receive fair trials with compensation being left up to the jury without unreasonable limitations. It was, then, up to the Plaintiff's bar to take that opportunity and translate it into care of their clients. *[Author's Note: In a surreal turn of events, West Virginia became a red state and the Supreme Court was in shambles. In the past few years at least 2 Justices were convicted of crimes, and another resigned before impeachment. The Governor's appointments to fill the positions until election included lawyers with no experience, and/or they had close business connections. It is a far cry from when the Court was esteemed by the entire legal nation. A new election was just completed. Only time will tell what will happen].*

Don Wilson was offered a seat on the bench for a year to fill out the term of another Justice. He would not accept the appointment unless Stanley agreed, and Stanley had no problem or reservations. Loss that it would be, Stanley could easily see the benefit to him and the firm of having a highly respected former Justice as a partner, and, either way, he would not have stood in Don's way under any circumstances. Don did serve on the Court, and the firm became known as "The Law Offices of Stanley Preiser." When Don returned in 1977, waiting for him was a large office suite and letterhead again bearing the firm name of Preiser and Wilson.

One could tell early Stanley would be an entertainer of some sort. circa 1932

Older brother Buddy and Stanley. circa 1933

Younger brother
Jerry. circa 1940.

In front of the
Oney St. house.
Stanley, his father
Joe, and brother
Buddy. circa 1940

Dependable, rough and ready All State lineman # 66 Stanley Preiser in 1943.

Attending the University of Chicago in 1945.

Stanley (2nd from right) would in later years almost qualify as a professional dice player. Here, it looks as if he is honing his skills. circa 1946

Demonstrative evidence as to why Stanley had the reputation of a party boy at the University of Virginia. circa 1947

September 6, 1948. Wedding day for Stanley and Joyce. They would slice their last cake together 60 years later.

The Wedding Party (l to r): Joyce's cousin Saul Loeb, Buddy Preiser, Joe Preiser, Alvin Preiser, Madeline Preiser, Stanley, brother-in-law Lionel Garner, Joyce, brother-in-law Eddie Kerman, Ben Monfried, friend Larry Padin, Rose Monfried, friend Marty Goldfarb, sister-in-law Carolyn Monfried, cousin Shirley Osen. 1948.

*Stanley teaching
at a trial lawyers'
seminar in Charleston,
WV. circa 1963*

*Stanley's press
photo. circa 1964*

Stanley stands behind West Virginia Governor Arch Moore and his wife Shelley as the Governor addresses the media after his 1976 acquittal.

Stanley and F. Lee Bailey at a press appearance. circa 1978

Stanley presenting the West Virginia Trial Lawyers Association award for Outstanding Legislator to Senate Majority Leader Robert C. Byrd. 1979

Stanley enjoying the perks of playing in a Pro-Celebrity Golf Tournament in Las Vegas. circa 1980

Stanley with Pittsburgh Coroner Cyril Wecht
after Dr. Wecht's acquittal. 1981

Stanley with
granddaughter
Blair recovering
from his heart
attack. late 1982

Joyce in her element with Wayne Newton in Las Vegas. circa 1984

Joyce reliving 30 years before with Paul Anka in Las Vegas. circa 1984

INTERMISSION

Howard Specter on the Man

> *Most people knew Stanley in only one or two compartments*
> *of his life – family, colleague, student, co-counsel, social friend,*
> *trial lawyers' groups, etc. I think only Dad's great friend Howard*
> *Specter, of Pittsburgh, traversed the entire landscape. Howard*
> *was a personal friend who became part of the family. He worked*
> *on cases with Stanley, was a student AND at times a teacher,*
> *devised educational programs together, drank together, dined to-*
> *gether, and thought together. Howard is a former President of*
> *ATLA, and was a legal counselor to this writer. What he writes*
> *below captures who Stanley was as much as anyone can.*

There were no elephants, bands, or clowns leading a parade along the avenue. The circus was not in town. Nevertheless, the denizens of Grant Street, the main thoroughfare in the center of downtown Pittsburgh where the State and Federal courthouses are located and the conclave of lawyers plies its craft, knew that something was afoot.

Stanley Preiser, or, "that lawyer from West Virginia," was trying a case. His reputation preceded him here, as it did wherever he appeared in court. Dapper. Smooth. Quick-tongued. Mean. Gentle. Hard. Soft. Even courtly. A former boxer. Incisive in questioning. He was all of these things. Whatever the moment and setting required. Not at all false. Just highly honed. The Swiss Army Knife of trial lawyers. He could pivot from being soft and gentle with a witness to cruelly eviscerating him and leaving him behind to bleed on the floor.

Lawyers jostled for seats alongside court personnel who scheduled their breaks to observe the man at work. It was never time wasted. Whether it was the defense of a real estate developer accused of fraud (a cheap competitor's dying gasp, Stanley called it), the cause of a public official charged with wrongful use of public property (a political foe's vendetta), or a murder for hire prosecution (a "simple contract case," he told friends), the legal community lined up to observe. As a friend and colleague, I was privileged to be there. His expertise went far beyond these criminal defense cases as he was also nationally known as a leading personal injury and wrongful death advocate in the fields of malpractice, product liability, and the entire gamut of civil litigation.

Stanley knew the rules, the exceptions to the rules, the exceptions to the exceptions to the rules, and the lore of trying cases. He did not feel constrained by the lore or by what others saw as practical "rules." Some say, for example, the first "rule" of cross examination is "Don't cross examine unless you have to or unless a witness harms your cause."

Stanley's view was that every witness should be questioned, however gently or for however short a time. He believed that jurors might see a failure to ask even one question as a sign that the witness was harmful. Similarly, some say the first rule is, "Don't ask a question unless you already know the answer." Stanley, however, said, "Don't ask a question unless you are prepared to deal with any answer." When he cross examined antagonistic witnesses, he was deft and laser like – no words or motion wasted or unplanned. He eschewed the notion that cross examination questions should be written out in full. There might be an element of theatre in a trial, but the script should be left behind.

Stanley made it look easy, but it wasn't. He often said, "I may not be smarter than the other guy, but I'll work harder." That was only a half-truth. I watched and worked with Stanley. He did work harder – harder than anyone I ever knew. But he never really believed the other guy was smarter.

As a long-time friend and colleague, I learned that Stanly knew there was more to lawyering than trial and appellate advocacy. He recognized and practiced the role of counselor in the truest sense. I saw him carefully, thoughtfully, and sensitively advise clients on legal points and the advantages and pitfalls of various courses of action.

Beyond legal niceties, he sought to bring peace of mind to troubled clients. He gently told the seriously injured, the criminally charged, or the client under investigation that he understood how difficult their situations were. He spoke of the mental and emotional burden and strain they bore. He expressed recognition that these problems would often be their last thoughts at night and their first awareness upon awakening. At the same time, he stressed that he was available and there to rely on. It was his job, he explained, to do as much of the worrying as possible and to absorb as much of the stress as the client would allow. He proved true to his word with his precept never to leave the office at day's end with a single client's phone call unanswered. No client stood alone.

[Author's Note: Howard Specter, who is writing this, practiced the same gentle and wise handling of his clients as did Stanley. I should know – he represented me in a business lawsuit, and his counsel in all the areas he mentions was invaluable].

Give me some men, who are stout hearted men,
who will fight for the right they adore.
Start me with ten who are stout hearted men,
and I'll soon give you ten thousand more.

Stanley Preiser was among the original stout-hearted men of the plaintiffs' bar. He adored the right to trial by jury, the right to just and honest recompense for wrong done, the right to representation by a strong, trained advocate, and the power in banding together to protect those rights. He, with a handful or others, began and carried on the battles to protect each of those rights.

More than six decades ago, he founded the West Virginia Trial Lawyers Association with a few other West Virginia trial lawyers to support and nourish those rights through state-wide education and practical training of the State's lawyers. A group of experienced lawyers who could have fit around a small dining room table conducted seminars in trial skills for lawyers thirsty to enter court rooms or to improve and build on existing skills. They taught on weekends and evenings years before even a single state mandated any type of continuing legal education. They taught in the cities and the towns – wherever someone was willing to learn and to join the fight for those cherished rights.

These men, led primarily by Stanley Preiser, grew to what is now an army of many hundreds of men and women who don the trial lawyers' armor to do battle throughout West Virginia and beyond. That fledgling Association today is recognized as one of the premiere trial bars in the country, and its annual meetings consistently draw the cream of the nation's trial bar as speakers.

In 1981, Stanley gathered an even smaller group to found the Melvin M. Belli International Law Society in honor of the original

King of Torts. Mel Belli was an innovator, teacher, and trial lawyer whose contributions to the cause were so great that Stanley said that every plaintiffs' lawyer was indebted to Mel for a share of every fee. I was privileged to be part of that initial group as a member of the first Board, and then the Society's third President. The Society was to be composed of ATLA members who had distinguished themselves as trial lawyers and who were committed to the international education of lawyers. Membership was by invitation and subject to Board approval.

The Society grew, and consistent with Stanley Preiser's vision, ultimately participated in international exchanges with local lawyers and jurists in Italy, Germany, Israel, Cuba, the United Kingdom, South Africa, Poland, and elsewhere. These meetings resulted in the publication of the group's International Law Journal. The Poland seminar included a meeting with Nobel Peace Prize Laureate Lech Walesa. In Cuba, members met with Ramon Castro. And in Israel, Prime Minister Begin. The highlight of the program in Italy was a Papal audience. What more could one ask? Or say?

The original stout-hearted few gathered by Stanley Preiser have become a true army in the cause of justice.

ROUND ELEVEN

Lead-Up to the Arch Moore Trial

In 1982, at the behest of friends and family, Stanley sat down to write about his life. He was never really comfortable doing so, and therefore only finished approximately 8,000 words about the events leading up to the Governor Arch Moore trial.

I began this book with a "teaser" about this case, which was, until that time, and perhaps still is, the most famous criminal case in West Virginia history. It was also followed closely nationwide. What you have below is not only Stanley's recitation of the facts from events that occurred only six years before his dictation, but, just as instructive, his analysis of the criminal justice system, at least as it was then. Few lawyers tried as many major criminal cases (in at least seven states) as did Stanley, so few are knowledgeable enough – or willing – to be truthful about a collection of laws and procedures that provides for little fairness to the accused, and allows for a great many abuses by the Government. Further, nothing Stanley says can be construed as sour grapes, because as far as I recall, and as my subsequent reviews of newspaper archives confirm, he only lost once, and that was overturned on appeal.

At the end of the chapter covering the Moore trial, I will interpose some commentary about matters we now know with the benefit of almost forty years of hindsight, and about occurrences that would have served as spoilers for the story if I related them as we went along. For example, one must keep in mind that as Stanley dictated these words and thoughts, Governor Moore was still a political force, having been able to serve out his term as Governor in 1977 after his acquittal, and being re-elected in 1985. Stanley and the Governor were very friendly during this period, and Stanley would have believed that when (if) his autobiography was published, Arch would see it. When you consider this, Stanley's courage to indict the Justice Department is quite laudable.

Stanley's Own Words

One day I picked up the telephone and the caller was Governor Arch Moore. What does a lawyer normally do when the Governor of his State calls him and invites him to join him for lunch? Of course, I accepted the invitation and met with him that day at the Governor's mansion, just across from the Capitol Building, where we were served a magnificent meal. Naturally, there was the chef with the white jacket, and the beautiful china and silver upon which we were served - but with Governor Moore there was no time off just to enjoy the food and its trappings.

The conversation began immediately by his saying to me, "Stanley, do you know what they are trying to do to me?" I responded, "I've heard the rumors on the street, Governor, and those of us who know you know that you are totally and completely innocent. We have done what we can to try to put a stop to those bastards over in the Federal Building."

Governor Moore then said, "Well, of course, there is nothing to this, but the rumors are flying hot and heavy. Is there any way to put a stop to them?" I was confident he wasn't fearful of a charge or an indictment because he knew he was totally innocent and that he would be cleared by trial if necessary. But you cannot defend yourself against rumors.

Being the courageous man that he was, he made the statement, "If they are going to do something, let them go ahead and charge me so that we can prove my innocence in a court room. But there must be some way to stop leaks out of the Federal Building. I thought that grand jury proceedings were private and confidential."

I explained that the rules do indeed provide that they are supposed to be private, secret and confidential, and only disclosed under certain circumstances. However, these rules are not followed by one side, and that is usually the Department of Justice, the U. S. Attorneys, and others working on the side of the prosecution. For some reason they believe the rules of ethics or law often do not apply to them as they apply to other lawyers. They frequently use the rules of procedure, as well as others, to their own advantage without regard to their true purpose.

Once in a while we can find a Federal judge with the courage and intelligence to enforce the rules even-handedly, but they, too, are few and far between, usually taking almost all representations of the United States Attorneys and the Department of Justice as true. The judges refer to those lawyers as the "Government" or "The United States," as if they represent all of us. As a matter of fact, instead of representing all of us, they represent damn few, and most of what they stand for and represent is not what the people want or believe.

But we've strayed too far from the story. Let's return back to the lunch at the Governor's Mansion. We began to talk about the rumors that they were going to charge the Governor with a criminal offense — either conspiracy, extortion, or some other concocted criminal charge.

To the uninitiated, as Clarence Darrow once said, we lost our freedom when Title 18, Section 371 of the United States Code was passed. They call it a conspiracy statute. Generally, it says that two or more persons who conspire, confederate or agree to commit a crime against the United States are guilty of a conspiracy, a felony, and can go to prison. And when you read the cases that have been prosecuted under this law, they are chilling and will make your spine hump-up like a cat, and the hair on the back of your head stand out, for you can be guilty of a conspiracy even though you don't know the other coconspirators, have never met them, or even though you may have never actually intended to carry out any statement you made.

After Arch told me the rumors were about conspiracy and extortion, I asked him if he had any idea what that meant, and he said he did not. I told him that word on the street had it that the primary accuser was Ted Price, himself under a multi-count indictment for SEC violations and other fraud involving a bank that had failed. I had heard Price was going to claim that Governor Moore said he would not allow Price to obtain a bank charter unless he first paid Moore $25,000.

This may be a good time to ask, who was this Governor Moore? Why was the Government, or, if not the entire Government, some of its representatives, out to "get him?" What and who were behind the rumors, and what was behind the actual, ultimate prosecution?

Well, to understand Arch Moore, a most brilliant and courageous man who undoubtedly was the best politician to come out of West Virginia, we need to know a little more-about his background. Arch Alfred Moore, Jr. was born in the little town of Moundsville, West Virginia, in 1923. When World War II came to the United States in the form of the attack on Pearl Harbor, he, solid citizen that he was, joined the army as an engineer, but due to manpower needs was transferred to the infantry.

In 1944, he received a disfiguring wound in the jaw from enemy machine gun fire in Germany and was left for dead for two days in a German farmer's beet field. When he was discovered, he was hospitalized and underwent surgery for facial reconstruction. Because of the bullet that had passed through his tongue, he was not able to speak for about a year after his wounding. Public speaking, a skill he would later exercise while holding office, was part of his physical therapy. Sergeant Moore was decorated with the Purple Heart, Bronze Star, Combat Infantryman's Badge, and European Theater of Operations Ribbon with three battle stars.

When Arch came home from the War he went to law school - West Virginia University - where he was one of the leaders of the class. He graduated and began to practice law, and in 1956 he was elected to Congress where he served very honorably for twelve years and earned the unlikely reputation (given his injury) as a powerful and persuasive orator. He then ran for Governor of West Virginia on the Republican ticket. West Virginia, like all the South of the day, was highly Democratic (in fact, in West Virginia the Democrats outnumbered the Republicans almost two to one), so for a Republican Governor to be elected is something of a miracle. But it demonstrates the personal magnetism of the man, which would later serve him very well at his trial during his testimony.

Arch took the helm of the Governorship of West Virginia in the year 1972. Now, there are those who accuse Arch Moore of being a controversial human being. I don't think that is really true. Those who exercise any degree of reasonable objectivity will see that he was truly a highly dedicated public servant, whose only interest was the good of the people of his State. Frequently, he would sacrifice his own personal well-being for the good of the people. He would work late at night, sometimes around the clock, on Saturdays, and on Sundays. I never knew him to take a drink or to walk away from his work at any time.

For Arch, being Governor was a twenty-four hours a day, seven days a week, fifty-two weeks a year business. But, as is usual when a Republican is serving with such distinction, leading Democratic newspapers began to attack him. They scraped into his background leaving no stone of his personal life unturned. Even when he practiced as a lawyer they found some activities which they claimed were questionable, and they began to print those lies and demand that the Ethics Committee of the State Bar investigate him for matters that were minor, very old, and very stale - things about which no one else would have been questioned.

Even the national investigative columnist, Jack Anderson, began to write about Moore - at times demanding that he be indicted for income tax evasion, and at other times ridiculously calling for an investigation of the same crime. That went on for many years and played a very major part in the story.

Now, what about this newspaper that first began to attack Arch so heavily in Charleston, West Virginia? Were they just following the Democratic *Washington Post* and Jack Anderson, or did they have their own axe to grind? The *Charleston Gazette* was one of the two leading newspapers in West Virginia, having the second largest circulation in the State. It began to attack Moore, report all sorts of rumors, subtly intimidate people appearing before the grand jury, and so on and so forth. These attackers included, quite incongruously, the Republican party chairman Tom Potter, who worked for the largest law firm in the State - Jackson, Kelly, Holt & O'Farrell, which Moore would hire in occasions when the State needed private counsel. It was beyond amusing and stupefying to me that the Governor would continue to let Potter and his firm do anything for him, because they also represented the *Gazette* in many matters, even though its defamation actions were taken over by another lawyer in the mid-70's.

The newspaper was so off base and so vindictive (the latter being a trait it never lost during Ned Chilton's years as publisher), that Governor Moore, and then many others, began to refer to it as the "Morning Sick Call" or the "Scandal Sheet." Again, these sobriquets followed the *Gazette* until Chilton left.

Who was Ted Price? I wish he were alive today so I could ask certain questions ruled irrelevant by the judge at trial, but he was unceremoniously killed in an automobile accident some years after the Moore trial. We do know that Price was born in another state, and came to West Virginia as a brainchild of some of the savings and loan institutions. He ultimately gained control of, and became President of, many savings and loan institutions. They built large edifices, and wanted to establish a bank in the Kanawha City area of Charleston. Price had the support of many of the city's leaders, who were convinced that he was a brilliant financial mind. Yet it came to pass that his entire empire collapsed, probably because of his mismanagement. He was not much of an executive, in reality. The best thing I could ever say about Ted Price is that he was simply a con man.

Well, the Governor and I had a very nice lunch that first day at the mansion. I told him that I could check around and most likely find out a great deal more about what was going on. As most of the better criminal defense lawyers around the nation have discovered, to survive and do the job for their clients it is necessary to communicate and have a pipeline of information from one to another. The F.B.I., the Internal Revenue, the United States Government, the Postal service, the United States Attorney's office, and all the rest of the government entities regularly work in harmony, after all, and innocent-until-proven-guilty citizens need a like conduit. The Government has vast sources of information, paid informers, hidden informers, people with new identities, witness protection acts, and all the rest designed to aid them in obtaining information. It was, and is, necessary, therefore, for the protection of the individual citizen that the good defense lawyers have access to the same type of thing. And, thus, defense lawyers of note would become part of an unofficial, yet valued, network.

Immediately upon leaving the Governor's mansion, I called some of these noted lawyers, many of whom were already representing various people appearing before the grand jury investigating the Governor. Even those who were not involved supplied some information, and some, involved or not, were just down right smart lawyers. I asked them all to feed information to me relative to these rumors.

All should know that the provisions of Rule 6E of the Federal Rules of Criminal Procedure provide that no imposition of secrecy as to what happened before a grand jury can be imposed upon a witness. Witnesses are entitled to disclose whatever they wish, and to whomever they want. The imposition of secrecy is designed to protect the reputation of people under investigation or, only if they desire, those who appear and testify. That is their decision. Conversely, it does prohibit the grand jurors, the United States Attorneys, the court reporters, and anyone else present, from disclosing information. Again, it does not control a witness.

In a case of this magnitude with its enormous publicity, the indictment began to look like a sure bet. In fact, remembering that the targeted Defendant is allowed no representation before the grand jury, it became obvious that they were going to indict Governor

Moore regardless of guilt or innocence. I was also convinced that they would indict him, if for no other reason, than to try and ruin him politically.

Ironically, it became apparent that the more innocent we proved Moore to be pre-indictment, the more likely it became they would indict. Why? Because the purer a defendant is seen to be, upon conviction the more points a prosecutor might score on his climb ahead. One cannot forget that most United States Attorneys and assistants have their eyes on another federal job, on a Governorship, or on a federal judgeship, and good publicity with indictments and convictions against bad citizens are the best way to put feathers in their cap. Reality does not seem to be a factor in the eyes of the Department of Justice, or of many United States Attorneys. Indictments of lawyers, politicians, and people of great prominence, that is their game – not guilt or innocence.

[Author's Note: Toby Vick, who ran several drug crime units for the U.S. Department of Justice, including the Miami drug crimes unit during the cocaine wars of the 1970's and 1980's, said, "There is nothing worse than an ambitious prosecutor, and most are ambitious."]

Due to all the publicity surrounding the moves of every person connected to the Moore case, along with the jealousy that seems to naturally exist between trial lawyers, I began to silently question whether I would really receive all the information I had sought. Would my colleagues start to help? Or, would this be the case in which the pipeline of information mentioned above would dry up so that one lawyer (this one) would not garner the expected extensive publicity in the most significant criminal trial in West Virginia's history, and/or might have his reputation tarnished with a loss?

I called the Governor several weeks later and told him I wanted to see him to report and advise him of several things. First, as every good criminal lawyer knows, the most dangerous instrumentality known to man is an invention of Alexander Graham Bell, which we now call the telephone *[Author's Note: Remember, Stanley was referring to 1975. I would say the progeny of the telephone may now have the "honor" to which he was referring.]* State and Federal agents can, and do, routinely eavesdrop on phone calls without search warrants or authority of any sort. Of course, sometimes with authority as well.

As a matter of fact, Assistant Attorney General under Nixon, Robert Mardian, stated in a speech to a legal seminar of which I was the moderator that there were over three hundred authorized wire taps in the United States. I interrupted him to ask, "Well, over three hundred might mean three thousand, or even three hundred thousand. Tell us how many there are." To which he responded, "Well, we really don't know." I had him admit, as we have had others admit, that very frequently the F.B.I. and other state and federal governmental agencies and organizations listen in on telephone calls, record, yet don't disclose it because they know they cannot use the information if it is obtained illegally. What they do instead is to take the illegal information and use it to find something they can legally use while keeping the illegal surveillance hidden.

And I also asked Mardian, "What happens if they are listening in on a lawyer and his client — what about the privilege?" The lawyer/client confidentiality assurance is the most precious and jealously guarded privilege we have in America. It protects the right of a client to tell his lawyer everything in truth, knowing that the lawyer, the good ones, the honest ones, will go to their graves without ever disclosing what was said. And no judge has the power, in most circumstances, to force a lawyer to disclose what his client has told him within this guarantee.

Yet Mardian (part of the Fascist-like Nixon regime) responded,

"Well, if the F.B.I., Internal Revenue Service, Postal Service, or whomever was listening in on this wiretap realized it was between lawyer and client, they were instructed to immediately abort the connection unless the lawyer himself was under investigation." That prompted the obvious question, which I put to him. "Who makes the decision whether the lawyer is under investigation?" Well, we all know the answer he gave, don't we? It is the person doing the monitoring. How many monitors or taps do you believe were ever turned off by these "great policemen?"

So, based upon what we knew, I told Moore to stay away from the telephone. I also told him to stop trusting his confidants and his official family (except his wife and daughters), and to stop sharing with his friends and political advisors any information that came to him, because today's friends could be tomorrow's enemies. They could turn into Government witness, because we all know that the Government buys and procures testimony by engaging in what is less salaciously called the plea bargain. But it is not so unusual, and those of us who know the rules and have been in the courtroom for over one-third of a century, know it to be true.

I explained all this to Arch and told him, too, about another horrible law known widely as "obstructing justice," Title 18, Section 1543. If you read it, you might be afraid to talk to your friend or neighbor. It says, in effect, that any person who interferes, intimidates or attempts to influence any witness before a grand jury or otherwise, is, himself, guilty of a felony known as obstructing justice. It is a highly misused provision.

This obstruction statute is what the Government uses to keep lawyers and clients who are under investigation from even talking to other people out of fear that if it doesn't amount to a conspiracy or a coverup, it will amount to an obstruction of justice charge. And I warned Moore about that. His response was curious. Having been a former Congressman who voted in favor of some of those laws, he pooh-poohed my caution. But he later came to find out the truth, and said to me that if he ever had a chance to return to Congress the first thing that he would do is try to correct laws that have been so misinterpreted and misused by the government in order to trample the rights of free people. *[Author's Note: Arch Moore's daughter, Shelley Moore Capito, has been in a U.S. Senator during the Trump years, and she has supported Trump almost 100% of the time as West Virginia's citizens experience huge health, education, and economic problems.]*

When I arrived, the Governor said, "Well, let's have lunch in the office today." A very delightful gentleman, Walter Ferguson, who had served so many governors, entered wearing his white jacket. He works only in the Governor's office, not in the Governor's mansion, which is across the street. I was ushered into the prestigious office where I had been many times with other chief executives, but Arch Moore brought such grace and honor to that position, and even to the physical office, that when you walked in it was almost like walking into the President's office, or a King's throne room. You knew that you were walking with one of the most dedicated public servants in West Virginia's history.

Lunch was served - a quick sandwich. As I said, with Arch Moore running the State was a twenty-four hour a day thing, and simply to have lunch and not talk about matters of great interest to the State or to the Governor was itself a waste of time to him *[Author's Note: Though he does not say it, Stanley shared this same work ethic.]* I suppose we inhaled the sandwich that day, because you have to continue talking business with the Governor while still chewing. He would not take the time just to eat the sandwich or drink the coffee. We talked about what I was going to do and what I had found out, and he made the central request at that point. He said "Stanley, will you represent me?" I responded yes, I would, and then asked why he had waited so long to formally ask me. He said "Well, first I don't know your politics. Secondly, this is a highly political trial. And thirdly, you know that if you take me on then you, too, will become the target of the 'Morning Sick Call' and others."

I responded that I had been attacked before, and being the target of the "Morning Sick Call" would just put me into a very esteemed class. But I told him as well that if we win, he and I will not only become a further target of the "Morning Sick Call," but of all his enemies for a long time to come - the United States Attorney's office, the political opposition, and whoever else was behind this vicious prosecution which was unjustified from its inception. Further, I let the Governor know that I expected to be attacked by the Internal Revenue Service again, having been examined by them more than once in the past. Good lawyers who have the courage to take a tax case against the government on the criminal side will, themselves, no doubt be investigated. In this way the Government hopes to dissuade able attorneys from standing up to them.

[Author's Note: Stanley defended numerous major tax cases, both civil and criminal. He held, as you recall, a Masters in Tax from New York University. He was also audited or questioned by the IRS more times than I can recall in an effort to "get" him or "dissuade" him from handling future cases against them. It was a given, then, that he took advantage of all that was legal to reduce his payments, and he was never cited for any illegitimate or improper activity.]

What did I then tell the Governor I learned thus far? Well, some very strange things. First, my fears about my colleagues were not well founded. The defense lawyers indeed came to my aid, which is akin to coming to the aid of Governor Moore. I found that many of the top lawyers in West Virginia felt that Moore was honest and a great public servant, and so they wanted to help. They thought that the government prosecution was founded solely upon one thing - the desire for the then United States Attorney for the Southern District of West Virginia, Jack Field, to become a United States District Judge (his father before him had been, and now his father sat on the Fourth Circuit of Appeals - the appellate court for the states of Virginia, West Virginia, Maryland, North Carolina, and South Carolina).

I gave the Governor all this information and told him I had arranged with Chester Lovett, an excellent and courageous lawyer who was representing Ted Price, to debrief Price and find out what he was going to say, or had already said. Also, George Daugherty had arranged for us to interview his client, Roger Baird, who ran Price's failed S & Ls for the Receiver after they all folded. Further, Jack Huffman set up an interview with witness Nolan Hamrick

Wheeling's Jeremy McCamic, who, in my opinion, has the finest legal judgment of any lawyer I've met outside of my partner, Don Wilson, represented the then Attorney General of West Virginia, Chauncey Browning, whom the government had subpoenaed. He, too, permitted me to talk with Browning.

In a side skirmish, I had also represented General Browning for a long time, and the Government complained about a conflict of interest and wanted me removed from the case. This conflict charge could only hold water if Browning was going to testify against Moore. We didn't know yet what Field wanted from any of these witnesses or, as it follows, just what Field was going to ask them. It was all secret. Oddly enough (and this I am sure will be a shock to you because it was a great shock to my wife who has been "practicing law" with me for thirty-two years - not as a lawyer but as a confidant - and whose judgment is superb), we have greater rights in the civil arena than we do in the criminal. Can you believe that in a civil case you get full discovery so you can learn what every witness is going to say by putting them under pre-trial oath and asking them questions? They cannot then vary from that testimony without risking peril.

You can file interrogatories (questions) to the other side and require their answers under oath. You can get a list of witnesses and be told briefly which each will say so you can decide if you want to depose them and learn more. You have a right to talk with every witness under oath and obtain copies of every document of relevance. *However*, when it comes to a criminal case, the federal judges are few and far between who give you any more than what the law just basically requires, which is almost nothing. It is almost impossible to get a witness list, it is almost impossible to get copies of documents in advance unless they were taken from your client, it is almost impossible to talk with witnesses, and you can't see the grand jury testimony.

Indeed, there is a storehouse of relative information all available to the United States Prosecutor, none of which is available to the defense lawyer until after a witness testifies. You can only imagine the scramble in the courtroom trying to read pages of documents in about ten to fifteen minutes (about the time most judges permit) before you must cross examine on that material. As I have alluded to, the system is totally designed not for honesty, not for integrity, not for justice, but for only one thing - for conviction of anyone charged by the United States Government. Who has the courage to say one is not guilty when the United States Attorney has signed an indictment that says you are? Statistically, many, many innocent people have been sent to prison.

As things go, in the Moore trial we had a pretty reasonable and fair judge who had been sent from another state after all the federal judges in West Virginia recused themselves. He reasoned correctly that if the U.S. Attorney could not tell us what the conflict involving myself, Browning, and Moore might be, he couldn't credibly argue I should be removed from the case. Skirmish over.

I again warned Arch to be careful about the law firm that was representing the *Charleston Gazette,* and to be wary of Tom Potter, the Republican Chairman, who was monitoring what was going on over at the grand jury. At that point I accepted employment, but only upon the basis that the Governor promise me that he would do exactly as I said. There were to be no public pronouncements, and it was to be understood that the very first time he violated my rules, my regulations, or my instructions, then I would no longer represent his interests. He readily agreed to that arrangement.

In a way, while Arch A, Moore was the Governor of the State of West Virginia, I was going to be the "Governor's Governor," or he would have to obtain another lawyer. As it came to be, though I become the "Governor's Governor" to all on the outside, between us the gloves were off. For example, the night before he took the witness stand the slugfest was so great that the walls of my inner office shook.

Those who were there that night heard the screaming hundreds of feet down the hall – especially from me, when I told Arch he was *not* going to make what amounted to campaign speeches while he was being examined. I instructed him to concentrate about walking straight and proud to the witness stand, answering that he would be truthful in a forceful voice, looking at the jury, and telling his story shortly, briefly, concisely, precisely, and to the point. He was going to answer the questions I asked, and not going to editorialize, and he was not going to philosophize. There would be no political speeches.

After some browbeating, Arch quietly said, "Stanley, if I simply answer just yes or no, I may very well hurt my future political career."

I then felt I had to cut to the core, and said, "Governor, if you answer your way and sound like a politician, truth or otherwise, you'll not have a chance to run for Governor again, nor any other political office, because you will be inside the prison walls. If you tell the truth, short and sweet, yes and no, and nothing else, you will go free because you are totally innocent. The world knows you are innocent. Even the prosecutors and the U.S. Attorneys and those at the Department of Justice, in their souls, know you are innocent. Innocent. Why make a political speech to take a chance? The Democrats on that jury might think that you are nothing more than a politician, but you are a Statesman, you are honest, you are innocent. Let's act like anything other than a politician." *[Author's Note: And that is exactly how Arch testified.]*

Again, I move too far forward. Let us digress to our lunch in Moore's office. After discussing the obstruction of justice statute, the conspiracy laws, and their misuse by the Government, and telling him not to talk to anybody because the government would then try to bring those obstruction of justice charges, Arch brought to my attention an old income tax dispute for which they had been investigating him for years. It was, he said quietly, raising its ugly head again.

One of the Governor's very good friends in Washington was also one of America's finest criminal lawyers, Bill Hunley. He had been handling the tax case initially. I told Arch I would be glad to work with Hunley in Washington on the tax case, but I also had a continuing thought. Perhaps Bill could open doors in Washington, legitimately to be sure, that were available to only a few. I thought we should ask for a conference with Richard Thornburgh, assistant

Attorney General for the Justice Department's Criminal Division, to discuss whether or not this horrendous bribery prosecution, which was totally unjustified, could be stopped by someone a little higher up in the government and more honorable than Jack Field. After some discussion, Arch and I concluded this was a good idea and he should get in touch with Hunley.

Before I left the Governor's office that day, Arch and I studiously looked around to see what kind of bugs someone may have planted. One can't be too careful. For example, the State Police are the Governor's security officers but it is not unusual (nor unjustified) for them to work in conjunction with the federal authorities from time to time. But who knew when? Who knew which side who was on? You couldn't tell the players without a program. So, we looked around for the bugs. We found none. Still, there is no doubt in my mind that many of our conversations were recorded by someone. I decided to find out where some bugs might be.

After I left the Capitol, I went back to my office (which is one of the locations we think had been compromised) and set up a fake meeting with known criminals with nefarious backgrounds — because I knew the Government would be very interested. The next day, Chester Lovett and I sauntered over to a very well-known public intersection downtown, and don't you know who we saw when we arrived? None other than our "ole friends" Fannigan, Bennigan and Itskowich, otherwise known as the F.B.I. I wish I could say I was surprised.

Several nights later I received a call at home from Bill Hunley, a most charming gentleman. It is easy to understand why few juries could ever find one of his clients guilty. He charms them to death at the same time as he intellectually convinces them. In any event, Bill and I talked about meeting with Mr. Thornburgh and decided that, if he was able to set the meeting, I would come over a day in advance to explain the facts to him, and bring some briefs of the applicable law. We were in accord that he should do the talking at the meeting.

Things at home were getting hot and heavy. Rumors were flying faster than sound, it seemed, and Field's office had "invited" the Governor to appear before the grand jury, even though he knew the Governor would not do so at my instruction. That is usually the final part of the attack as it permits the United States Attorney to make sure the grand jury knows of the refusal and associates it with guilt. As an aside, no lawyer with any experience allows his or her client to testify before the grand jury. Had Nixon and his crowd not testified, they probably would never have been indicted. *[Author's Note: Just as if Trump had testified before the House it is doubtful the Senate could have acquitted him on certain charges.]* When they call you before the grand jury as a target, they have evidence that makes them believe you are guilty. If you testify you are not, they indict you for perjury, and if you testify you are, they indict you for the substantive offense. There is no way to gain anything by appearing under these circumstances.

On the morning I was to go to Washington for our Department of Justice meeting on the extortion (not the tax) case, when I tried to stand up, for the first time in my life I fell to the ground. I got up again, and fell. Got up once more with the same result. I awakened my wife and told her I had to take that plane in a couple of hours, but I knew that I was very sick and probably had a raging fever. It was indeed 104°.

I called a good friend/doctor of mine and told her I had to be on a 10:00 airplane. It was now 7:30 and she had to do something to control the fever and dizziness so I would be able to navigate. My wife drove me down to her office. There I received two shots of penicillin and a number of penicillin pills, and off I went to the airport, still almost unable to navigate. But I arrived in Washington about 11:00 and was able to meet with Bill Hunley late into the night organizing the material.

We went to meet with Mr. Thornburgh the following morning. Guess who else showed up. John A. Field, III, the great prosecutor who was going to make his reputation and pave his way to a federal judgeship on the scalp of Arch Moore. We sat down in a large room in the Attorney General's office at the Department of Justice Building, and in walked Mr. Thornburgh with his entourage. He sat down, and Bill asked him to please tell us what the charges against Governor Moore are purported to be.

Even though people believe that the Government needs to prove you guilty, that's all hogwash. They often won't even tell you what you are charged with. Instead, Thornburgh asked if we had a defense to present or wanted to show him why there should be no charges or indictment at all. Tell us!, he practically screamed. We answered that if they would tell us what the charges are, we will prove them untrue. They refused to tell us anything, accusing us of only attempting to obtain some free information to which they felt we were not yet entitled.

After a while we became exasperated. And we asked what ever happened to the great American Constitution? What happened to the presumption that all men are innocent until proven guilty? And if we are innocent, how do we know what these charges are?

Well, the reality is that the Government will not concede the Constitution – to them your client is not innocent, s/he's guilty. Across the land nowadays, you start out with the presumption of guilt, not only with the Department of Justice, but with the jury and spectators. All good trial lawyers know the presumption of innocence has been dead and buried ever since Bobby Kennedy became the Attorney General of the United States. He was singly responsible for the total corrosion of the protection of the rights of the individual, and the rest of the prosecution and police have picked up on it.

Bill Hunley labored on and made a tremendous presentation. Again, no objective person would have permitted an indictment to be returned against Governor Moore in light of the evidence we presented. We left, and the following morning, showing how much consideration they really gave to our petition, I received the telephone call, the inevitable telephone call, from the United States Attorney saying they were going to return an indictment against Governor Moore within the week.

By now it was nearly Christmas and I asked Jack Field, "Well, I'm sure you will wait until after Christmas or the first of the year?" I'll never forget the response of a man obsessed. Field said, "Stanley, Arch Moore is going to receive the damnedest Christmas present he ever received in all his life."

Low and behold, he was predictably prophetic, for on the 2nd day of December the Grand Jury returned an indictment against Arch A. Moore, Jr. There were no statutes of limitations or other time deadlines - they could have just as well waited until the end of January. But the United States Government was determined, acting through their overzealous prosecutor, to give Arch Moore a gift for the holidays he would never forget.

Between the time we had decided to go to Washington and actually went, we scrounged and scuttled around to amass all the documentary evidence possible to prove this entire matter was nothing more than a political witch hunt. I thought of what they did in Salem in 1776 to witches, and concluded they never stopped the burning — innocents are still at the stake in political trials.

So now we approached one of the great political trials of the century. I knew it was political, I knew the intent was to get Arch Moore so that someone else could become Governor of West Virginia, but I had not yet figured out how to make the public accept that as fact. How can you convince good, solid, honest American citizens that the United States Government is composed of people corrupt enough to knowingly indict an innocent man in order to advance the political ambitions of a prosecutor, or the political ambitions of someone of the opposite party? It's true — the great lawyers of America know it, but the public does not want to believe it.

I, too, did not want to believe that President Nixon could be a crook, or that his cabinet or the Attorney General of the United States, John Mitchell, could go to prison. None of us want our institutions proven to be corrupt. But we live in a society where guilt or innocence is no longer of any significance. And I knew it. So, I began to try to bring the kind of proof to the public that would exonerate an innocent man, for sharing it with the Government was a worthless and unwinnable situation.

It is very difficult to prove your innocence when you don't know what you are being charged with. So, with my associate Mike Farrell at my side, we had to examine every facet of Arch Moore's life. What possibly could the Government be focusing on? Was it really a charge of bribery for a bank charter? Was it spending political money or contributions and reporting incorrectly? Was it a conspiracy to violate state laws? Were the postal authorities involved? Was there a mailing that they would claim involved some criminal act? Was it the use of interstate facilities like a telephone to carry on the proceeds of a bribery? Were they claiming a conspiracy? Was it an income tax evasion case? What was the government trying to prove? We just did not know.

We needed to start preparing for trial even before indictment, however. It is so. Believe it or not, the government can take years to investigate and finally indict with the help of hundreds. Yet, the Defendant will be forced to trial in usually three to six months, and without the help of anyone but his or her lawyer and the lawyer's staff.

Well, we had "nothing" to do other than prove that every act in the life of Arch Moore that was not barred by the statute of limitations, that is, not outlawed by the passage of time, was itself antiseptic and pure. This, itself, was a Herculean task. We put that case together and brought it to the Government, of course, to no avail. But, when we brought it to the jury and to the people of America through the free press, it was a different story.

ROUND TWELVE

The Moore Trial and its Aftermath

The stage was now set for a true spectacle. Except for West Virginia Mountaineer football in good years, it is doubtful any singular statewide event ever garnered as much newsprint, or held the attention of as many interested citizens, as did the trial of Arch A. Moore, Jr. Stanley was ready to go, as was his second chair, Michael Farrell, mentioned earlier. But every other lawyer and law student in the office was on call.

As you have seen from Stanley's own words in his run-up description, any conviction of Arch Moore would require the jury to believe that Ted Price, head of Diversified Mountaineer Corporation (DMC), secretly gave the Governor $25,000 ($115,750 in 2020 dollars) to obtain a bank charter while visiting Moore's private office in 1972. Jack Field was confident he had plenty of proof of this – too confident in the opinion of some. Nevertheless, following his opening statement, commentary could be heard that it looked bad for the Governor, given all the evidence and witnesses Field promised.

Experienced lawyers and court watchers have seen it before - a criminal case that looked impossible to defend at the outset being totally dismantled by a superb defense lawyer. And the irony always is that after defense counsel does his or her work, so many lawyers and much of the press will fail to give the defense lawyer the recognition due. Instead they take it easy on the prosecution and opine that even though the evidence was slight, the U.S. Attorney did well with what s/he had. Even jurors sometime believe the defense had an easy job winning what was really a difficult case. Naturally, they only heard actual testimony, and not the proffers, puffing, and bragging as to what was expected.

Stanley believed in the jury system and the role an oath (and the perjury charge that went with it if one lied) would play in causing a witness to tell the truth in Court, even if s/he had made contradictory statements beforehand. He also believed it was up to defense counsel to try and help the many witnesses who were badgered and threatened to lie by the Government. These ordinary citizens would need courage to come forward with the truth, and Stanley always attempted to make the truth sound like an inescapable conclusion to bolster their confidence in speaking honestly.

The seven-man/five-woman jury was empaneled some time during the week of April 19, 1976. Whether it was a smart move or not, Field called Ted Price very early in the case. The direct examination was rote and relatively boring, but it did bring into evidence that Price claimed his pay-off meeting was arranged with the Governor thru Nolan Hamric, a banker from Gassaway, West Virginia, and a friend of Moore's. According to Price, Hamric suggested that a "campaign contribution" would get Moore's attention about the charter Price was pursuing. Price said Hamric called Moore's friend and co-Defendant Bill Loy to make the final arrangements for the meeting.

Price also testified that Roger Baird, Comptroller of DMC, came up with $30,000 and gave it to him to give to Moore. According to

Price, he then went to the Governor's office at the appointed time with $25,000 in $20 bills in three brown, letter-sized envelopes. He said that Moore directed him to transfer the bills from the envelopes into a cloth draw-string bag about four feet in diameter sitting on a table in the middle of the office. Price never said on direct examination what happened to the other $5,000.

That was pretty much the extent of Price's testimony – it was to the point and ended late one afternoon. Stanley would have to wait overnight for his cross examination. As experienced trial lawyers will attest, whether it be a civil or criminal case, little turns on the juices more than the anticipation of destroying the other side's main witness(es) on cross examination. One of the lawyers in our office compared Stanley that evening to a dog who had not had meat for a long time. He was figuratively salivating to get started, not only on Price, but on Baird, Hamric, and others who Jack Field believed were going to back up what turned out to be an impossible story concocted by Price. Remember, Stanley thought the truth was inescapable.

Without going through the concessions and proof adduced by the witnesses in chronological order, what follows is a summary of how Stanley shot down the Government's case, much of it through his vaunted cross examinations. Even lay people are familiar with the so-called "rule" of cross examination that an attorney should never ask a question to which s/he doesn't know the answer. From the early days of his practice Stanley taught and lectured that the construct was too simple, and even promoted laziness. His point of view (which might be more universally used 50 years later): "Never ask a question on cross examination to which you cannot handle the answer."

You will recall that in the preceding chapter, Stanley wrote about the unfairness of not being able to see many pieces of evidence or the Grand Jury testimony *before* trial. *After* Price testified, his Grand Jury testimony transcript, taken under oath, was finally provided to the defense. Stanley was shocked to learn that in front of the Grand Jury, Price had described *three* visits to Moore. Of course, this was in direct contradiction to Field's opening statement and Price's testimony at trial. As we would come to learn, about six weeks before trial Roger Baird explained to Field that a one visit scenario at the time Price claimed would have been impossible because $30,000 was not available to Price on that day. So, they *changed the story* to include only one later visit with $25,000 divided between three envelopes. It is unlikely Price did this on this own. It is more likely he had some Government help in fashioning this lie to this jury *[Author's Note: Yes, this implies Mr. Field was dishonest – wait for the end of the story.]*

When Roger Baird testified, he also gave greater detail about the money situation. He claimed on the stand that Price had said he needed $30,000 to obtain the charter, so Baird arranged for him to have the money. Price was the boss, and Baird was an employee, but Baird said he was concerned that the funds might be for illicit use.

However, Baird then testified that the money was never used for anything. He said he personally deposited $20,000 of it back into the bank. Stanley suggested Price stole the other $10,000 for himself. In a later twist, Price's secretary would testify that she drove Price to the Capitol at a different time of the year than when Price had maintained he went to see Governor Moore. This left the door open for Stanley to opine on summation that Price took some of that $10,000 to pay off someone other than the Governor for some other purpose.

In an effort to salvage his contradicted testimony about the pay-off money, Price testified that he had indeed taken $25,000 to

Moore, but instead of three meetings there was only one, at which Price delivered those three payments at one time in three different envelopes containing $20 bills. In a stroke of genius, Stanley obtained the judge's permission for him to ask Price to fit $25,000 in $20 bills into three envelopes. Stanley then arranged for the money to be delivered from the bank in open court, of course knowing what the result would be because I had spent the evening before trying to make the money fit (Looking back, I'm surprised Stanley didn't say, "If it doesn't fit, you must acquit"). When Price was unable to fit the cash into the envelopes, he said that he must have had some of the money in his pocket when he met with Moore, or he must have forgotten that he had been carrying a fourth envelope. But by then, the goose was royally cooked and stuffed.

Nolan Hamric had testified that there was some innocuous communication about a campaign contribution and a charter, but on cross said he never imagined it had any connection to Moore. People give contributions to politicians all the time with the expectation of a little access – nothing wrong with that. The crime is contributing for a specific purpose to receive something specific in return. Further, campaign contributions were limited and required to be reported.

At the hour Price said the call was made to set up the meeting with the Governor through Bill Loy, Stanley had learned that at that time Loy had been in an important meeting. Stanley called a dozen people who were in that meeting to the stand, and each one testified Lloyd never took a call or left the room.

Stanley also called as a witness every employee that worked in or near the Governor's office, including State Troopers who are always present when the Governor is in the building. They all testified they had never seen Price.

Price ultimately conceded to Stanley that the persona he cultivated in 1972 as a rich executive was a ruse. He admitted he took trips to London, the Greek Isles, the Virgin Islands, borrowed $50,000 from a DMC Board Member to give to his wife, and bought his girlfriend a $4,000 ($18,500 in 2020 dollars) ring in New York. He admitted he was in debt by $200,000. Finally, Price agreed that he and his girlfriend had set up a business where they stole money due client investors and spent it on themselves. And how much money did they take? A little over $25,000. Stanley jumped on that number and suggested this was the money Price claimed went to Moore, but, in reality, Price had spent it on personal trips and jewelry. According to Richard Grimes of the *Charleston Daily Mail*, Price tried to deny it, but, by that point, no one was listening to him.

Grimes also reported that Price held up rather well under Stanley's withering cross examination for a good portion of the day, but as the grilling went on Price's exasperation began to show. At one point, Stanley questioned him about recalling dates from only the week before. To that, Price answered, "At this moment, I'm not even sure what day it is now."

At Stanley's insistence, direction, and example, we were always well prepared and our files were well marked. However, they were marked in code so no one would know what we had. Early in the trial, we noticed someone from the Government, usually when things were sort of casual during recess, sneaking a peak at what books or files were on the defense table.

Thinking we might have a little chuckle at their expense, we began to label some dummy files with case names that had nothing to do with any issues at this trial. Sure enough, we started to see lawbooks on the opponent's table containing the cases we had written on the files. That meant the U.S. Attorneys were spending their time and resources researching issues and trying to figure out what we had up our sleeve, not learning until later that we never intended to rely on those cases. It was all clean fun, and they never complained, but it reminds me of the famous poker game in *The Sting* where Paul Newman switched cards on Robert Shaw, who himself was using a marked deck. After Shaw lost and his henchman asked him what he was going to do about it, Shaw exclaimed, "What do you want me to do, report him for cheating better than me?"

As for the trial itself, the day came when all that was left for the attorneys to do before the jury would deliberate was to deliver their closing arguments. It felt as if all of Charleston tried to cram into the courtroom that day. I don't think Stanley ever gave a better summation, but by that time he had some good material to work with.

During the testimony it had been revealed that Price had made a plea bargain with the Government to receive favorable treatment as it related to some upcoming Securities Fraud charges. You will recall that Stanley called out this particular practice in his own recitation above as akin to paying for testimony. He also alerted us that U.S. Attorneys' concerns are primarily about scoring political points for convicting politicians, and not so much to do with the quest for justice. This spectacle seems to have proven Stanley right. There was no evidence produced that Governor Moore was in any way a crook, yet there was a mountain of evidence heard by all that would easily gain Price that title. Nonetheless, the Government was willing to let Price's conduct slide in an effort to lasso the higher-profile Moore.

For me, and for those to whom I have spoken who were present at that trial, two defining moments stood out against the rest of Stanley's summation. The first came while he was speaking of Price's buying expensive jewelry with what was probably stolen money.

Stanley wore with pride some of the tributes he received from admiring and grateful clients. He enjoyed telling the stories of what came from whom and why. For example, years later a grateful divorcee gifted him his frightfully expensive gold Cartier watch after Stanley won a healthy equitable distribution from her wealthy governor ex-husband (not Mrs. Moore).

He also wore a gold and diamond pinky ring given to him by Jimmy Petite, the Morgantown coal magnate, after Stanley successfully defended him on criminal charges. Stanley liked to tell the story that he was Joyce's mother's favorite of all her sons-in-law (Joyce had three sisters). Not only was he Rose's favorite, he said with a nostalgic look on his face, but he was the only one of them she felt she could truly trust. She told him that when she passed, she was leaving him $10,000 to buy a stone. Then, with a glint in his eye and a comedian's timing, he would hold up his ring, polish the diamond on his sleeve and ask, "Like it?" He only told this story in front of Joyce, and even though everyone knew he was kidding, it drove my mother crazy.

So, during summation this heavy gold and diamond pinky ring flew off his hand and into the jury box when he waived his arm around while talking about Price buying jewelry with stolen money. The ring actually hit one of the jurors.

Dad always contended he did this on purpose, but I know he would never have risked injury to the jurors or faked something to get what might be improperly close to them. I think he was a bit embarrassed, so he turned the mishap into a purposeful scheme to get close to the men and women in the jury box by asking them to retrieve his ring. In this way, it became a good story, too. I love my Dad and I know he might be watching me write this book, but I have to say I have never fully bought into the truth of his particular account of the scene.

The second moment came at the very end of the summation, and in Stanley's mind may have been the theme of the defense which he was waiting to drive home at the most opportune time. He stood before the jurors, looked them in the eyes, and proclaimed, "Arch Moore is a powerful Governor and presence. If he had really been given $25,000 to procure that bank charter, you, and everyone else, can be sure it would have been issued . . .It wasn't."

When the verdict of acquittal was announced, the courtroom burst into cheers. The Court tried to quiet things down quickly, but there was too much pent-up emotion that needed to escape. Once decorum had been established, the Court gaveled adjournment. The path from the jury box to the exit took each juror past the Governor, who shook hands with every one of them. Dozens of well-wishers followed with congratulations. And finally, the Marshals and State Police escorted the Moore family and Stanley out of the building where Arch stopped to make an impassioned speech to the local and national press about Government abuse and the beauty of the jury system.

The U.S. Attorneys, within a minute of the final gavel strike, had vanished. Go figure.

Our team went back to the office for a relaxing round of cocktails (Arch had coffee, as I recall) and chit-chat. There were congratulatory calls and telegrams coming in for Stanley by the dozens from all over the country. After a while, the Governor and his family, who must have been exhausted, said their thank-yous and good-byes, and left for the Mansion. For them, this ordeal was blessedly over. For the team and all the lawyers, a night of celebration was ahead.

Mike Farrell, who, after two years with Stanley, which would be like four anywhere else, expounded on the trial in his own words:

When the federal government indicted the Governor, a war of wills ensued. First, the Feds set up telescopic listening devices across the Kanawha River in an attempt to eavesdrop on the conversations ongoing in Stanley's personal office. How did we know this was happening? The State Police, who at least overtly were loyal to Moore, had teams of troopers following the teams of FBI agents who were preparing the case. This surveillance tag scenario repeated itself every time I went to meet with a witness or prepare the Governor for trial.

The theory of defense seemed simple, but it was not. Price alleged that the exchange occurred in the Governor's executive office. To enter that office, a visitor must go through a receptionist. Price was not listed in the Governor's Appointment Book. None of the receptionists could recall his entering or leaving. The Governor denied the transaction. The FBI executed a search warrant for the contents of the Governor's desk.

Joseph Young, the Baltimore Federal District Judge appointed to try the case, was a plus for the defense in that he was fair and impartial. The search warrant was specific to cash, and there was plenty of it — $250,000 was found and seized. The Indictment charged that only $25,000 had been extorted. Judge Young ruled that the fruits of the search warrants, the $250,000, were inadmissible unless the Government could prove that $25,000 of the total came from Price. Ultimately, the Government could not segregate the alleged Price money.

Lie detector usage was rampant. Every witness on the Governor's witness list was invited/subpoenaed to the U.S. Attorney's office and offered a polygraph exam to prove that s/he was telling the truth, or expose himself or herself to a perjury count. Several witnesses flunked the government polygraph and hired a private polygraph operator. Some witnesses had as many as five pretrial polygraphs. All testified, and none were indicted for perjury.

Stanley was concerned about the "half sentence political speak" that the Governor used to communicate. He tasked me to meet with the Governor on a daily basis and change his speech pattern and sentence structure. These sessions consumed six weeks.

By the time that trial began, the stage was set for a national clash of federal versus state with Stanley and the Governor being the lead story on every nightly newscast. Every day, six bankers' boxes of our possible exhibits came and left like clockwork. Stanley perceived himself to be a legal surgeon in the Courtroom. The exhibit boxes held the scalpels. Another Rule — produce every exhibit from the box within five seconds of receiving the request or do not get out of your chair.

Next Rule — the Defense Team could never look unprepared to the jury. Stanley was committed to the proposition that persuasiveness was the byproduct of intense preparation and supreme confidence. You could be bold and courageous but never stupid. As a public figure, the Governor had to convincingly deny the accusation for us to win. The same was true for co-Defendant Bill Loy. Stanley selected civil defense lawyer, Ed Eardley, as Loy's counsel even though Eardley had never tried a criminal case. I was the baton carrier in this joint defense communication channel. Eardley went to bed between 5:00 and 6:00PM and arose at 5:00AM.

Stanley rarely left the office during trial before midnight. Thus, near midnight Stanley would teach me his trial plan for the next day, I would sleep four hours, arise at 4:00AM, and teach Stanley's plan to Eardley.

The night before the trial began both sides accessed the (confidential) National Crime Information Center (NCIC) Computer Database to determine whether any of the jurors had criminal records. One did. Once seated in the Courtroom, the Prosecution asked for a bench conference at which they complained that the defense had accessed the information base. Judge Young listened intently and then asked the U.S. Attorney how he discovered the defense's use of the NCIC computer. Jack Field responded that the government had also accessed it. Judge Young took control of the trial at that point and ordered both sides to provide all NCIC records to the Clerk and not to use the information learned in any way.

The trial was uneven in its intensity. Going through twenty-seven receptionists and security witnesses, all of whom denied seeing Price in the Governor's office, was necessary, but very slow and monotonous. It paled in comparison to some of the time when the Governor, Loy, and Price were on the witness stand. The sketch artists had a field day capturing the high points on their canvases. Two of these artists were twin sisters who worked for competing networks (NBC and ABC). They sat side by side but never spoke to each other.

We survived a last ditch failed effort by Field to introduce the $250,000 contents of the Governor's desk drawer, and also the mystery as to who endorsed a $5,000 check from a Milton Nursing Home operator that the Feds unsuccessfully tried to link to the Governor.

Closing arguments spiked when Stanley gestured so violently that his pinky ring flew off and hit a second-row juror in the chest. Eardley's laconic closing consisted of a series of rhetorical questions as to why Bill Loy was a defendant when he was barely

mentioned by the witnesses. Seven hours later the foreman an-
nounced NOT GUILTY. In typical Stanley fashion after ev-
ery successful trial, his office was transformed into a Speakeasy.
Victory was sweet and well-earned.

I'm the first to concede that what occurred years after the trial
(described below) sounds like the improbable ending to a bad novel,
but, as they say, truth is often stranger than fiction.

After his exoneration, Arch Moore went back into politics and
the public eye, being elected Governor again in 1984. He was beaten
by Democrat Gaston Caperton in 1988. In 1990, after an extensive
federal investigation, Moore stood before a judge to answer charges
of five felonies, including mail fraud, tax fraud, extortion, and obstruction of justice.

Though I have never told anyone until now, I was present when
Arch met with Dad about representing him in these later charges.
Stanley was hesitant to take on the second Moore case for two reasons – he lived in Florida by that time and was not looking forward
to reliving this kind of long battle. Second, and just as significantly,
Arch had never made a good faith payment of even a single cent
toward his 14-year-old legal tab.

Dad and I discussed the options (not that he really needed me), and
Dad turned the case down. What he would never tell me was what he
learned about the actual substance of these new charges from Moore in
a private meeting ("Monty, would you go get us some sandwiches for
lunch?"). As far as I know, Stanley honored the privilege, and never told
anyone what he and Arch discussed that day one on one.

Arch pled guilty. For these crimes, he was fined $3.2 million,
though he paid only $750,000 after reaching a settlement. He was sen-
tenced to five years and ten months in prison. Of this sentence, Moore

served two years and eight months in federal prisons in Alabama and Kentucky and four months home confinement in northern West Virginia. He attempted to withdraw his guilty plea by blaming his lawyers (not Stanley) for bad advice, but was never successful.

Jack Field and I got along pretty well until I saw Price change his story about delivering the alleged money to the Governor in one trip. But, as is probably no surprise to anyone after learning Field "gifted" the indictment to Moore during the Christmas season, he had always been cold and lacking in empathy. My most memorable personal experience with him was when Jack came to our offices for a pre-trial mutual exhibit exchange. As we were taking care of business he commented, "Isn't this great? It's going to be a lot of fun." The kind of a remark speaks for itself.

Field had been expected to win the Moore trial. After taking a beating from Stanley, however, Jack's career sort of stalled. And in 1998, the old adage of "what goes around comes around" was played out in Newark, New Jersey, when Field pleaded guilty just before Christmas to racketeering and conspiracy charges in a telemarketing plot that cheated investors out of $80,000,000. In hindsight, it isn't very far-fetched to think that he probably had a hand in Price's fluctuating testimony during the Moore trial.

The United States Attorney in Newark, Faith Hochberg, who prosecuted Field, was quoted in a 1998 news article as saying, "From a career full of promise to this day, [John Field III's] admission of guilt is evidence of the rock bottom of his slide from protector of the public to predator on the public." Faith later became a federal judge, and almost 20 years later by some miraculous coincidence, Sara and I happened to be sitting next to her and her physician husband at lunch on a 2019 cruise. We parlayed that into dinner, and, as you might imagine, the conversation was anything but boring.

ROUND THIRTEEN
June, 1975 – March, 1981

Soon after the verdict in the Moore trial I graduated from law school, took a couple of weeks off, and prepared to begin formal employment at the Law Offices of Stanley Preiser, soon to become Preiser and Wilson. In those days, if you graduated from the WVU College of Law you were not required to pass a Bar Exam to practice in that state. In theory, this made sense, because there was only one law school in the state, and it focused on West Virginia law and procedure.

Thus, if the professors passed a student one would naturally conclude s/he should be qualified to practice. And WVU attracted some pretty good professors – Thomas Cady, Vincent Cardi, Patrick McGinley, Frederick Schauer, Paul Selby, Franklin Cleckley, and law school dean, Gordon Gee. Dr. Gee went on to fame as the President of Ohio State and Vanderbilt Universities before returning as President of WVU, where he sits today.

In reality, however, in years to come WVU grads were no longer allowed to simply graduate and enter practice —- not after money reared its head. Continuing Legal Education had become big business by the 1980's, and the West Virginia State Bar Association was missing out on the dollars. By instituting a required Bar exam and offering Bar Review courses, the organization fed its desire for more money. However, as I said, when I came to the Bar, I was able to enjoy my summer instead of preparing for another test.

Little did Stanley know that my appearance would trigger a challenging chapter of his life, and it revealed a good deal about him. Every time a young lawyer joined the firm s/he was at the bottom of the totem pole, so to speak, in terms of office location and furnishings. The firm had a great number of lawyers by then, and was continuing to grow. I was cognizant about my being "the son" and wanted nothing special. Dad was on the same page, knowing any other course could lead to various problems. But there was the proverbial "fly" in the office ointment.

Joyce Preiser, as you know by now, was no wallflower. She began to work on Stanley behind my back, advocating for me to have a better office and amenities. In my mother's mind, there was an undeniable difference in my employment and that of others – I was the son. To avoid a war, Dad devised a compromise. One day unannounced I was moved to probably the second-best location in the office, which satisfied Joyce. But it is an understatement to say that my furnishings left a little to be desired. This apparently also satisfied my colleagues, who were mostly great people, and seemed fine with how all it worked out. I knew nothing of these behind-the-scene maneuverings until many years later, but leave it to Stanley to balance taking care of his family with the perfect "settlement."

Paraphrasing Mike Farrell, Stanley was now the toast of the national criminal defense bar. Maryland Governor Marvin Mandel was under indictment, and Stanley was asked to become lead counsel. The case fascinated Stanley because of the national notoriety it had attracted. The Moore case had been a one count indictment, but Mandel was charged with forty-four counts that included federal racketeering allegations. Stanley ultimately declined the case as he foresaw better uses of the firm's human and financial resources than to handle a multi-month federal trial in Baltimore.

The next major battle for Stanley would take place in November of 1976 in the little mining town of Welch, West Virginia. Legend has it a former President once described Welch as the "armpit" of the world. Stanley represented Rodger Morgan in a medical negligence case against the local hospital and two local physicians. No lawyer in the Welch area would touch the case – not only because the defendants and the hospital provided health care for everyone in McDowell county, but also because the area had never seen a six-figure personal injury award. The case came to Stanley, who tried it with Alvin Hunt. It would be the first medical negligence case I worked on and sat through from beginning to end.

Roger Morgan had suffered injury when his brain was deprived of oxygen during what was alleged to be a botched spinal tap. The actions and subsequent inactions of the defendants were, plaintiff alleged, below the general medical standard of care (what a reasonable person can expect a reasonable doctor to do or not do under certain circumstances). At the time, however, West Virginia sill clung to the antiquated rule that a health care provider's standard of care was to be judged on a local basis (what a reasonable person could expect a doctor to do or not do in Welch, West Virginia). By this definition, practically *any* care could be deemed adequate locally. This made it almost impossible for plaintiffs to find expert medical witnesses because most courts did not permit out of town, much less out of state, experts to testify about local standards, and no local doctor wanted to testify against a colleague.

As a small-town judge who did not have many opportunities to preside over civil cases of note, Judge Jack Marinari relished this one, and did a masterful job. Stanley praised him both during his summation and for many years to come. Judge Marinari agreed with Stanley's argument that the medical standard of care should be the same locally as it was nationally. All doctors, he reasoned, take standardized tests, and so the standard of care should be the same everywhere – in other words, the local standard equaled a national standard. Accordingly, the judge permitted one of the world's leading brain surgeons to testify in Mr. Morgan's case. The courageous Dr. Yale Koskoff had been a pioneer in helping the public obtain top-notch medical care by his willingness to testify to the errors of others in the medical profession.

After weighing Dr. Koskoff's testimony against those of the defense witnesses who claimed Mr. Morgan had no brain injury at all, the jury found against the hospital and its staff and awarded Mr. Morgan $350,000 in damages, which equates to about $1,620,000 in 2020. Soon after the Morgan case, which was never appealed, the West Virginia Supreme Court relaxed the barriers to out-of-state testimony in these types of cases. This was a significant change that would benefit the West Virginia justice system and its people as a whole.

In 1977, Justice Don Wilson returned from his temporary place on the West Virginia Supreme Court. His steady, guiding presence, and his fine judicial work over the past year, added even more luster to the firm, which had grown to a point where there weren't enough large cases in the Charleston area to pay the overhead – Preiser and Wilson needed to officially go national.

Stanley's first trial that year was *Anderson vs Marshall County (West Virginia) Cooperative*, to be tried in northern West Virginia. The case involved serious injury sustained by Kenneth Anderson when an allegedly defective roto-tiller exploded. The law in product liability cases was unsettled nationwide. The plaintiff sued both the seller and the manufacturer of the roto-tiller, but obtaining verdicts for plaintiffs was difficult in cases like this for three primary reasons. Firstly, there was no direct contact between the manufacturer and the user. Secondly, it was difficult to prove that a manufacturer acted unreasonably when making a product. And thirdly, the seller claimed simply to have been a middle-man, so to speak, and had no responsibility for a product that it did not make or alter.

Stanley saw this case as an opportunity to move West Virginia towards adopting strict liability. *[Author's Note: Unless a lawyer was attending quality legal education programs, it is unlikely s/he would even know about the trend nationwide toward improving this area of the law.]* Under a strict liability theory, a manufacturer is responsible for injuries caused by its defective product no matter how much care was used to make it, and regardless of whether the manufacturer and buyer had any direct contact. Strict liability also makes sellers of defective products responsible for injuries because they profited from the sale, even though they did not manufacture the product.

Ably assisted by Joseph Zak, now a family court judge in Charleston, Stanley successfully convinced Stephen Narick, a gutsy trial judge, to apply the advanced legal standard advocated, and the jury returned the first million-dollar verdict ($5,000,000 today) in West Virginia history.

Of course, the Defendants' insurance companies had no interest in giving the West Virginia Supreme Court the opportunity to officially refine product liability law in this progressive manner. They understood the dangers to their bottom line if strict liability became the standard all over West Virginia, and opted to settle the Anderson case instead of taking an appeal and rolling the dice on future cases. Primarily due to this thinking, product liability law in the state went without change for two more years.

But the manufacturers and insurers could not escape the

inevitable when Federal Judge John Copenhaver asked the state Supreme Court to clarify West Virginia law on strict liability. Judge Copenhaver was considering the standard in our case of *Morningstar vs. Black & Decker*, so he sent the issue directly to the State's High Court by way of a "certified question." Though I was actually handling the case for Preiser and Wilson, a number of better researchers than I (Joe Zak and Ted Kanner taking the lead), wrote much of the brief advocating the West Virginia Supreme Court's adoption of strict liability. Naturally, Stanley and Don added their thoughts and directions. In 1979, Stanley argued the matter before the Supreme Court and the new, progressive standard was indeed adopted as state law, finally putting West Virginia on a par in this area with other states in the country that had considered the question.

William Parsons, a former President of the West Virginia Trial Lawyers Association and a fine, very successful trial lawyer from Wheeling, remembers seeing Stanley for the first time, and working with him a few years later on a product liability case. He recalls, in his own words:

> *My first memory of Stan Preiser was during a trial demonstration while I was a law student at the West Virginia University College of Law in 1973. I had heard his name mentioned, but had no idea who he was other than a tort lawyer from Charleston. After the first five minutes of Stan's preliminary remarks, I knew I was in for something extraordinary. That raspy voice, the wavy silver hair, the piercing steely blue eyes, and his boxer-like stance as he addressed the audience was mesmerizing. By the end of the demonstration, after he had manhandled the expert neurosurgeon, I also knew that his skill had to be that which every student should emulate.*

Coincidentally, when your author saw this note from Bill, it reminded me of something that had occurred later that same evening. I was a member of Bill's law school class. The program had been moved to the county courthouse due to the number of students and local lawyers who were expected to attend. That evening, about 6 students tagged along with the lecturers for dinner. Stanley, as was his nature, said he was picking up the bill.

One of the other lawyers said he would pay the tip, which was not small since the meal was almost unlimited, but Stanley refused. Later, I asked why? I mean, how many times have we all enjoyed drinks or dinner with someone, picked up the bill, and let the "other guy" pay the tip to save a few dollars? A very common occurrence. Not this time, and in answer to my question Stanley advised: "Never let the other guy pay the tip – he thinks he paid his share."

But back to Bill Parsons' narrative:

Little did I know that just four short years later, after graduation and moving to Wheeling to begin my general practice of law as an associate with Jerry and Jolyon McCamic, I would be co-counsel with Stan in a products liability case against the Crossman Arms/Coleman camping equipment company. Jerry had associated Stan on the case and I, as a young associate, was asked to tag along. I was elated.

I quickly got to see the master at work. The defendant Crossman was the designer and manufacturer of an air rifle that we alleged put out the eye of our young client due to the negligent design of the rifle's safety mechanism. Our theory was that when our client used it, the safety was of an old design that was later corrected. We contended it was the defective design that caused our client's rifle to discharge while the safety was engaged.

Crossman's "Director of Safety and Design" was the first deponent, and Stan tore into the young man immediately with those "zinger" first questions he would hurl at a witness who was expecting to at least be asked his name before being interrogated. The questions were relentless, rapid fire, and probing, all without the aid of notes or an outline. Stan was always prepared.

After a while, the Safety Director started to become evasive. Stan, acting outraged, but in complete control, turned to me and said, "Bill, call Judge (Callie) Tsapis and tell her I want to convene a Grand Jury and indict this man!" Who was I to not do as I was told? I looked up the judge's number, and began to dial. Stan, knowing full well that he couldn't demand the judge to convene a grand jury, stopped me. He knew from the terrified look on the deponent's face, however, that non-evasive answers would be forthcoming and his bluff had done the job.

Later in the deposition, Stan, while questioning the witness, was waving the gun (unloaded) around and happened to briefly point it at the witness. This poor, beaten down guy raised his hands over his head in surrender. Stan smiled and said, "Don't worry. I won't shoot you," to which the defeated Safety Director responded, "You might as well, Mr. Preiser, you might as well."

On April 27, 1978, disaster struck the little town of Willow Island, West Virginia, located on the Ohio River about 100 miles north of Charleston. Fifty-one men were on scaffolding building a cooling tower for a power plant when the scaffolding, which was attached to the tower, pulled away. All 51 men fell 170 feet to their death.

A first group of three widows engaged Stanley to represent them based on the advice of local friends the firm had represented in the past. The next group came at the behest of attorney Bob Goldenberg, who you may recall was the last surviving founder of the West Virginia Trial Lawyers Association. As usually happens in mass tragedies, there were numerous meetings amongst the families to determine the best way to proceed. David Stuart of our firm was masterful at gaining the confidence of most of the aggrieved ladies, and Stanley, primarily with Dave's help, would end up representing the vast majority of plaintiffs at a fee ¼ below the usual.

Steve Brill, owner of the *American Lawyer* news magazine, flew from New York to West Virginia to write a story on how the lawyers were hustling clients, taking big fees, and mistreating the widows. After his visit, interviews, and other investigation, Brill instead wrote a most complimentary article about Stanley's ethics, legal abilities, accomplishments, and reputation. He also wrote about how much Stanley's clients trusted and liked him. Stanley was always very proud of, and flattered by, that article.

The cases took a few years to complete, primarily due to attacks the defendants made on each other, as well as the obligatory claim that the deceased workers had done something wrong themselves to cause their fall. There were huge fights amongst the defendants over exactly what had gone wrong and who was to blame. Did the manufacturer produce defective concrete that failed to hold the scaffolding to which it was attached? Had the concrete been mixed properly by the vendor who delivered it? Were there adequate warnings on the concrete packaging about the water content and the time the concrete needed to set before a rain? And, did the workers fail to use the proper bolts to attach the scaffolding to the tower.

The cases ultimately settled in about 1982. I don't know the precise figures, but David Stuart told me recently that after only the first round of settlements he left the courthouse in St. Mary's with endorsed checks for about $7,000,000 (approximately $19,000,000 in 2020 dollars). He jokingly says he doesn't know why he ever returned to the office.

It was during this time period that Stanley began to think flying commercial was taking up too much of his time. To rectify that, he and cousin Alvin Preiser, with whom Stanley had "protected" FDR 40 years before, and who was now President of Preiser Scientific, formed SCAT airways and purchased a private plane. Craig Pearlman, my college roommate who had become the youngest flight instructor in the country at age 18, and who taught me to fly while we were roommates in college at Tulane in New Orleans, also had gone to law school and moved to Charleston to practice with the firm. He became both aviation advisor and trusted assistant to Stanley on various commercial cases.

Craig, now practicing law in his hometown of Orlando, FL, still credits Stanley as the "cornerstone of my personal and professional success." Craig also came up with the best line about what superior preparation can do for you at trial. *"When things got squirrely, and it appeared that Stanley 'pulled a rabbit out of the hat,' it was because we had 50 hats and 50 rabbits. We were always ready for anything."*

Though hard to fathom now, in the late 1970's and early 1980's there were very few successful women handling cases in major plaintiff's firms in this country. Stanley decided to do something about that. Barbara Fleisher Allen, who became one of *the* stellar attorneys in West Virginia and Pennsylvania, puts it this way:

> *I first met Stanley Preiser in 1976 when he came to the West Virginia law school and asked to meet the first winner of the Stanley E. Preiser Scholarship – me! After we talked for a time, Stanley announced that I would be the perfect person to*

"integrate" his law firm: "We need a woman! We need you! And we'll wait (since I still had two years of law school ahead of me)!" This was all pretty heady stuff, since Stanley was already a legendary trial lawyer whose name was spoken in hushed tones by law students.

I assumed that Stanley would quickly forget this conversation, but as I later learned, he never forgot anything. Anything! Had the phrase "steel trap mind" not already been in existence, it would have been necessary to coin it in order to describe this brilliant man. Sure enough, two years later he sent his plane to bring me to Charleston to meet "the gang," after which he informed me that it would be up to me to decide whether I was tough enough to break the high, hard glass ceiling existing in the field of trial law – historically, a man's field. The long and short of it was this: Yes, I told Stanley, I'm tough enough, but I need to know that you're actually going to train me to be a trial lawyer; I don't want to spend my career in a law library, hidden from view (which was the fate of most female lawyers at that time). The pact was sealed.

Stanley was true to his word. Knowing that my primary interest was in criminal law, he made me a part of his criminal team and gave me a real-world education in putting together a defense that would convince a jury of our client's innocence. I could not have asked for a better mentor and role model. He insisted that everyone treat me with respect – including judges, which took guts galore — back in the day when female lawyers were marginalized at best, and frequently treated with disdain by an entrenched legal fraternity and by old-school judges who considered us to be a lesser species. Within the walls of our office Stanley may have teased me about being a "lawyerette," but outside those walls I was his colleague, and don't you forget it.

I was second chair to Stanley in many big cases, and I think we made a pretty awesome team: he was positively magical in a courtroom, keeping the jury enthralled, the prosecutor off balance, and the witnesses eating out of his hand, while I was an efficient, organized sidekick who made sure that whatever he needed was right there. Mike Farrell discussed the "Five Second Rule." I like to brag that I could find what Stanley wanted before he even asked for it.

But Stanley, to his eternal credit, had bigger plans for me than second chair. I graduated to trying cases on my own, always with Stanley's full support and with access to all the resources at his disposal. He encouraged me to be myself, to face down hostile judges, and to wear the stiletto heels I love rather than the sensible shoes favored by the authors of Dress for Success. He was generous with his time and praise – always tempered, of course, with the reminder that, "I taught her everything she knows – but not everything I know!" When I won my first big criminal case, he closed down the office and held a party that went on for all hours.

Stanley was genuinely thrilled with the success of everyone in his orbit, but I like to think that he took special pride in bringing women into what had been a male-dominated club. I was the first woman at Preiser & Wilson, but not the last, and all of us owe a huge debt of gratitude to this lion of the profession.

While Mary Beth Ramey is perhaps the best know female trial lawyer in the country, she is also a great lawyer, period. She oversaw the ATLA educational programs for many years and has been honored numerous times for her successes in her home state of Indiana and elsewhere. Along the same line as Barbara's recollections, but more from a national perspective, she tells the following story:

Few people become legends during their lifetime. Stanley Preiser did. When I met Stanley in the 1980s, his national reputation as a winning, fierce advocate, both in criminal and in civil cases, was already well established.

Our first meeting was as faculty members for an education program sponsored by the American Trial Lawyers Association. While I was unaware at the time, I now realize that Stanley sought me out because he loved to teach and encourage other lawyers to achieve heights which they did not even know existed. To place my comments about Stanley in context, at this time there were very few women practicing law. The swashbuckling gladiator lawyers who identified themselves as trial lawyers were an exclusive community. This closed-door club was 99.9% male. Stanley, however, undertook the mission of providing me with educational tools that he felt I needed to open the doors of acceptance for women trial lawyers. He decided to become a mentor to me, which meant that he was going to challenge me to set and achieve goals which he saw for me that I did not even know existed.

Stanley once suggested to me that for a woman to be an effective courtroom lawyer, she had to wear a wedding ring. The size of the wedding ring had to be ¾ inch, and it had to be a plain gold band. According to Stanley, by wearing this plain gold band wedding ring solely on the 4th finger of her left hand, the woman lawyer achieved greater credibility with the jury. No diamonds. When I responded that many men did not wear wedding rings, he looked at me and very straightforwardly said, "Men don't have to. Men walk into the courtroom with credibility because jurors think that men are lawyers who know what they're talking about. If you are going to try to achieve the credibility your male

*opponent has, you must buy and wear the wedding ring that I
have told you to wear. Jurors notice."*

*As an icon of the trial bar, Stanley Preiser's influence in open-
ing doors for the female trial lawyer cannot be overstated. Because
of his reputation and persuasive nature, he unlocked and opened
doors for many who would otherwise never have been provided
the opportunity to actually achieve their dreams.*

In one of Stanley's most celebrated cases, he defended a northern West Virginia lawyer named Leonard Alpert on charges of
racketeering and conspiracy to commit the same. The indictment
also identified the Hancock County, West Virginia, Sheriff and the
County Prosecutor as taking protection money from illegal gam-
bling houses. The FBI had videos of all the defendants, and Alpert
was seen giving money to the Sheriff after a fake raid for the return
of some illegal slot machines.

The Sheriff confessed at the trial. The Prosecutor, represented by
well-known lawyer Rudy Ditrapano of Charleston, was convicted
and sentenced to thirty years in prison. Of the three defendants, only
Stanley's client, Leonard Alpert, was acquitted. In legal circles, since
the FBI had Alpert on tape, no one is quite sure how Stanley pulled
it off. But it added to the legend.

There is one more story from Mike Farrell he enjoys that further
demonstrates Stanley's breadth of experience. Mike recalls research-
ing and writing a brief for the Fourth Circuit Court of Appeals.
Stanley had won a $5,000,000 defamation verdict in Clarksburg,
West Virginia, against Irving Moliver, and Moliver had appealed.
Mike and Chip Calwell, another excellent lawyer and Preiser and
Wilson associate at the time, were assigned to research every ap-
pellate defamation case in the United States. When Mike turned in

his half of the brief and Chip announced that he was still writing, Stanley opined, "Chip, you are a lawyer, not an artist." Unfortunately, the verdict was ultimately reversed on appeal through no fault of the brief writers.

If there was one field of study that fascinated Stanley, it would be persuasion. He would studiously watch all the great orators of the day, whether he agreed with their message or not (for example, Billy Graham, who Stanley said could physically move an audience with the wave of a hand). He would also pore over writings to determine what held a person's attention. In writing briefs designed to persuade a judge or judges to adopt the ruling he desired, Stanley opined: "Rarely, if ever, use a footnote. This is not academia. Judges won't stop in the middle of your argument to find it, and if it is important enough to cite, it is important enough to be included in the flow of the point."

Beginning in 1979, Stanley and I began to teach the National College of Advocacy's Advanced Medical Negligence course. Twice a year, we taught together for 5 days at Harvard University and the National College of the Judiciary in Reno, Nevada. The medical part of our team was either the country's most recognized forensic pathologist, Dr. Cyril Wecht, or the equally famous come a decade later, Dr. Michael Baden, who as I write this was just completing the autopsy on George Floyd in Minneapolis.

The course, attended by lawyers from across the nation, naturally expanded Stanley's reputation (and it did not harm mine) in the medical negligence field. We taught this course together in 1979 and 1980, and I taught it for 3 more years with a great lawyer from Wichita, Kansas, Gerald Michaud. The exposure from teaching these sessions helped the firm immensely as it moved into the national limelight.

Elvis died in 1977. The Tennessee medical examiner, a friend of the Presley family, first concluded that the cause of death was a heart attack from hypertension, and that drugs had not played a part. Someone apparently thought they could hide The King's drug use by throwing out the contents of his stomach before they could be examined. For whatever reason, that person didn't count on a tox screen exposing the star.

In 1980, the Tennessee Medical Board brought charges against Elvis' private physician George Nichopoulos for overprescribing, and sought to suspend his medical license. Stanley was asked to consider handling the defense. After looking into the case, Stanley felt it was a winner but asked the opinion of all the firm lawyers about whether he should get involved. The time he would spend would be extensive and we would all have to pick up the slack. We really didn't need the publicity or more cases at that moment. I still recall the meeting in Dad's private office – all the lawyers were against it, but made clear we would back Stanley's decision. He declined, and, as he predicted, Dr. Nick (as he was called) was later exonerated.

By 1980, the advances in West Virginia law had made the state a preferred place for a plaintiff to file an action. In contrast, the Commonwealth of Virginia, whose laws West Virginia had adopted in 1863 when it became a state, was lagging far behind. In the medical negligence arena, Virginia had never had a verdict of any great size, and, as in the Roger Morgan case discussed above, Virginia held tightly to the old "same or similar" locality rule as the test for medical expert testimony. You may recall this meant that an expert had to be from the immediate area where the alleged negligence had been committed, or from a community almost exactly like it. Since doctors refused to testify against other doctors they knew, it made it almost impossible for a plaintiff to obtain competent experts and win.

After hearing Stanley speak at a Trial Lawyers Association meeting, Jim Minor of Richmond asked Stanley to associate with him in what anywhere else might have already been a very large malpractice case. Observing one of his first cases as a new lawyer in Minor's firm, and relating the events here, was Lee Forb, who would soon after leave Richmond to work for Stanley.

As had occurred in the Morgan trial in West Virginia, Stanley persuaded the Virginia trial judge to go beyond the antiquated "same or similar locality" rule and allow physicians from other states to testify that modern medical training was the same everywhere, and so the community where the negligence occurred was the same or similar to theirs. This resulted in one of the first plaintiff's medical negligence verdicts in the state, and certainly the largest.

Not long after Lee Forb came to Charleston, he and Stanley traveled to Logan, West Virginia, to represent Mr. Taylor, who had been seriously injured in a car wreck. The defendant Wolf carried insurance limits that were, in Stanley's opinion, enough to settle the case. With the approval of his client, Stanley demanded the company pay those limits.

The insurer refused to pay, despite, as we later learned, a recommendation from its own attorney that it do so. The verdict against Mr. Wolf was for more than he had in coverage limits, which put his personal assets at risk. In an unusual move, Mr. Wolf allowed Stanley (who had just sued him) to file a case against his insurance company for the overage. Stanley argued that the insurance company had failed to act in good faith and settle within the policy limits when it had the chance. Stanley and Lee were successful, as were a few other West Virginia attorneys who were, at that time, advancing the same theories for their clients. These "Bad Faith" cases have been upheld by the courts and are commonplace today, but Stanley was one of the first to pioneer this important concept in West Virginia.

In early 1981 Stanley spent time in Zanesville, Ohio, where he successfully represented the former County Prosecutor in an attempt by the Ohio State Bar to suspend his license.

In another matter over with before it had a chance to become public, Ted Kanner tells the story of a very prominent West Virginia professional who had not filed tax returns for many years. Ted and Stanley traveled out of state to meet the Government agents and lawyers in charge of this investigation, and spent a good deal of time discussing the great harm that an indictment would do to their client. At the end of the meeting, Stanley made an impassioned plea based primarily on the goodness of his client and the many positive things the man had brought to the economic and cultural life of the community. The agent, who had no doubt heard these type stories before, was genuinely moved this time, and there was no arrest.

Bill Druckman, who started with the firm in 1981, became one of the state's leaders in the medical negligence field. He remembers his first such case, which was also his first with Stanley:

Shortly after I began, I helped prepare a medical malpractice case for Stanley in Wheeling. Our client had been diagnosed with cancer and treated with chemo, but she was actually benign.

When we got to the hotel and set up our war room, forwarding counsel and Stanley each tried to outwork the other with me walking between both elephants. My jobs were to finish an endless "To Do" list, and keep the Scotch glasses full.

After many hours of working and drinking, we headed out to eat. I had heard about Stanley's legendary appetite during trial preparation. He ordered a 16" pizza for himself, other entrees, and pitchers of beer. After this working dinner we stopped at a

store where Stanley bought a gallon of ice cream, and then it was
back to the war room to prep over Scotch and ice cream.
   Around midnight, Stanley wasn't feeling so well, and, obliv-
ious to my snickers, said he couldn't understand why. Regardless,
a couple of days later when the trial began, he destroyed the defen-
dant's expert pathologist, and then had our own expert psychia-
trist declare our client's injuries from the chemo were such that
she was incompetent to testify. The case settled by the end of week.

It was about this time that Stanley founded the Melvin Belli
International Law Society to honor the man Stanley and most lawyers of the day believed modernized the plaintiffs' bar. Mel was certainly the most famous lawyer in America from the mid-50's thru
the early 90's, and the Society now boasts over 500 of the best lawyers in the country. It has sponsored educational exchange seminars in, among other locations, Italy, Israel, South Africa, England,
Germany, Poland, and Cuba. The seminars in Germany, Poland, and
Cuba all took place before the "Wall" fell in 1989, and the Society
made a second trip to Cuba again in 2016.

Mel was a character, and had set the early standards for cer-
ebration and creativity among lawyers. When the New York baseball
Giants moved to San Francisco for the 1957 season, the city built
a new major league stadium at Candlestick Park. It sat on the Bay
where it was even windier and colder in the summer than downtown
San Francisco. To entice the wealthy to buy box seats for the season,
the team advertised that the box seats were to be heated. They were
not. Mel, who himself had purchased a box, sued the Giants and
won.

These were the days before free agency, and at that time players
were considered chattel, essentially meaning they were the property

forever of the team that drafted them. When the Giants refused to pay Mel after his victory, he decided to "attach" the greatest Giant of them all, Willie Mays. In other words, Mel essentially claimed Willie Mays as his own in satisfaction of the judgement. Meanwhile, there was still no heat in the boxes, so Mel informed the team that he would not allow Willie to play so long as it was still cold. The team installed heaters the next day, Mel pronounced that he was warm enough, and Mays went back to center field.

In 1984 Mel invited six American lawyers to join him for a week as guests of the Cuban Government. The trip ostensibly was for the purpose of sharing ideas about the two countries' legal systems. In reality, both sides had other motives. The Cubans only wanted to propagandize, and it turned out that Mel and Sidney Bernstein, then the Society President, were on a covert mission for our Government that the rest of us initially knew nothing about. To this day, we have never discovered the specifics of the mission, but it had to do with certain get-togethers with religious dissidents. We learned about it after the meetings were completed, and on the next to last day on the Island. There was some trepidation among the other five of us about getting home, I can now safely report.

The Cubans had to approve the lawyers who would visit, and Fidel's brother, Ramon, singled me out over cigars and rum to discuss animal husbandry. He owned a cattle ranch and assumed I raised cattle because I was from in West Virginia. The gulf between us was wider than the language barrier, and it didn't help that I didn't smoke.

One night we made a visit to the famed outdoor Tropicana Nightclub in Havana. While watching the entertainment, one of the lawyers asked Mel how he liked the show. Mel happened to be sitting next to me, and after three or four seconds of hesitation he said, "Well, Monty is not bad company, but when I was here 30 years ago, I was with Errol Flynn and he talked six chorus girls into going home with us. I'll tell you tomorrow how much I enjoyed myself after I see how much like Flynn the young Preiser is." In the end, I had a great time, but I'm afraid Mel had a lousy evening.

Stanley hosting Harry Philo, President of the
Association of Trial Lawyers of America, and Governor
Jay Rockefeller at Stanley's office. circa 1984

Look out, it's Captain Stan. circa 1985

Stanley's press photo. circa 1985.

Stanley, Broadcaster Howard Cosell, and the author
at a WV Trial Lawyers Seminar. circa 1986

Joyce's sisters and husbands (l to r): Stanley, Joyce,
Lionel Garner, Shirley Garner, Florence Kerman, Eddie
Kerman, Carolyn Wolf, and Si Wolf. circa 1996

Your author and wife Sara. circa 1997

Three of Stanley's closest friends, Howard Specter,
Elaine Specter, and Robert Volpe. circa 1997

Grandchildren Blair and Justin Preiser at
Stanley and Joyce's 50th anniversary party. 1998

Cruising was a favorite activity for Stanley and Joyce. 1998

Stanley and Joyce at their 50th Anniversary party. 1998

*Stanley and Joyce with close friends and cousins Alvin
and Gayle Preiser at 50th anniversary. 1998*

Stanley enjoying the Fishbone Fred years. circa 1998

AL JOLSON ENTERPRISES, INC.
11½ 17TH AVENUE SOUTH

MASTERLINK STUDIOS 24 TRACK

CASSETTE EXPRESS

ASA JOLSON RECORDS

JOLIE HOUSE MUSIC, ASCAP

AL JOLSON
BLACK AND WHITE MUSIC, BMI

SWANEE RIVER RECORDS

Stanley visiting headquarters while President of the Al Jolson Society. circa 1999

Always popular among the younger set, here Stanley and Joyce dine with friends and colleagues Gregg Rosen, Monique Rosen, and George Mahfood at Stanley and Joyce's country club. 1999

Stanley and Joyce with unidentified friend on a tour to Israel with the Jewish Federation. circa 2000

Always the boxer, this is a favorite stance of Stanley's as he delivered a speech. circa 2001

Long-time friends, colleagues, and great lawyers Gary Gober of Nashville and John Romano of West Palm Beach presenting Stanley with the "Mel" Award in 2003, given to one attorney each year who best embodies the nation's trial lawyers.

*Stanley and
Joyce headed to
the dance floor
at the Melvin
Belli Society
dinner in 2003.*

*Stanley hosting Joyce's 80th birthday party,
January 27, 2009, at Arturo's, just 11 months before
he went to plead cases for those in the afterlife.*

ROUND FOURTEEN
April, 1981 – mid 1986

Throughout the late 1970's and 1980's there were a series of cases involving cars with automatic transmissions that would slip out of park and into an immediate powered reverse. This change in gear would happen without warning, and cause injury or death to scores of people who were struck when hit by a vehicle someone "knew" was in park.

We took on one of these cases against Ford, to be tried in federal court in Huntington, WV. When we got involved, much of the evidence needed to prove the defect had already been discovered by others. However, the evidence was not black and white, and the automotive behemoths, including Ford, were digging in their heels against settlement. Statistics showed that about 10 of 13 cases had been lost by the plaintiffs nationwide, and any settlements that had been reached were for meager amounts. Our case was filed in the late 1970's and concluded in late 1981 or early 1982. As was so often the case, Stanley's involvement resulted in a significant advance in the way these cases would be presented going forward.

First, at the behest of fine Alexandria, Virginia, lawyer Bernie Cohen, Stanley engaged Bob Brenner, a mechanical engineer from Maryland, as an expert witness. Brenner had been with the National Highway Traffic Safety Administration (NHTSA) during the late

1970's while Democrat Jimmy Carter was President. This was a time of concern about the safety of motor vehicles which led to many safety initiatives that became vital to the American driving public's protection (think Ralph Nader). When Ronald Reagan was elected, and the Republican administration's focus shifted away from concern for individuals and more toward protecting industry, Bob left federal employment and began his own consulting firm near Rockville.

Bob constructed a see through plexi-glass working model of a transmission which allowed him to demonstrate to the jury exactly what happened when the car slipped gears. His model became standard demonstrative evidence in these type cases from 1982 forward. He also provided a valuable history into long term complaints about this very problem. Brenner continued to speak the truth in various cases against manufacturers of many products despite threats to his own safety. His contributions in this arena deserve serious recognition.

Stanley obtained a $400,000 settlement (approximately 1.3 million dollars today), which was the largest settlement anyone had commanded from Ford. Fortunately for the public, this paved the way for swifter, larger recoveries for plaintiffs, and forced the automobile industry to do what common sense dictated they should have done out of the gate. They finally re-engineered the transmission system to fix the slippage problem.

Stanley's subsequent case was much different and had other significant implications. Except for a number of professional athletes, and maybe Mr. Rogers, Dr. Cyril Wecht may be the most well-known name in Pittsburgh and western Pennsylvania. Described by many as the most brilliant person they have ever met, Cyril was the elected coroner of Allegheny County. He holds degrees in law and medicine, and by 1980 was the most famous forensic pathologist in the country. From JFK to JonBinet Ramsey to Sharon Tate, Dr. Wecht has been involved as a private examiner or a television commentator on most, if not all, of the high-profile deaths in America over the past 55 years. In his professional capacity as County Coroner, of course, he also handled many cases in the Pittsburgh metropolitan area.

Dr. Wecht's energy and courage were boundless. He served as an expert witness in hundreds of cases nationwide, answering many medical questions within the broad confines of pathology. He taught lawyers and doctors, and founded the prestigious Pittsburgh Institute of Legal Medicine, composed of both professions. He was a prodigious writer, turning out articles and books at a stunning rate. He chaired and participated in numerous charities, and he had a large family to whom he was utterly devoted. There was not a major plaintiff's lawyer in the United States who did not know the name of Cyril Wecht, a man who could always be counted on for a fair opinion to be backed up with his personal testimony in court when needed.

With all the other responsibilities in his life, Cyril was also one of the most influential people in the Pennsylvania Democratic party. He had immense sway over voters, and there were many enemies who wanted to see him out of favor. So, when he came under indictment in late 1980, as so often is the case when great men come under fire, it was clear that strong political factors were in play.

Cyril's enemies and the prosecution team, which included James B. Lees, thought they had found a crack in the doctor's armor, and they were confident they could exploit it. They ignored Dr. Wecht's innumerable contributions to the community, to the state, to the nation, as well as the prestige he brought to the city of Pittsburgh. Never mind that there were millions of tax generating dollars that flowed through his private Pennsylvania company. Never mind that the training county employees received in the coroners's office, as well as his own, was far and above anything that the government provided. Never mind the inherent good of the man, himself, as a philanthropist, teacher, scholar, and friend.

Lees and the County still charged Dr. Wecht with theft of services. He was accused of using three county morgue employees to perform about $115,000 worth of tissue tests for his private firm, Pittsburgh Pathology and Toxicology Laboratory, from 1974 - 1979. If convicted, these less-than-exciting charges would brand Cyril a felon, wreck his career, and curtail his political influence.

Stanley's reputation and successes were well known to the legal community across the country, yet he employed no public relations firms to inform the public of his accomplishments. Stanley and Cyril had been friends for many years, but the newspapers were skeptical about the defense being in the hands of a West Virginia lawyer. Actually, there were two West Virginia lawyers — Barbara Fleisher, today Barbara Allen, was sitting second chair. By this time, Stanley rarely handled a major criminal matter without her help.

Yet the press were not the only ones to express doubts about Stanley's ability to win the case. His friends privately suggested that he stay away. Pittsburgh is across the border from West Virginia, and much of northern West Virginia can be considered part of Pittsburgh's metropolitan area. Stanley's West Virginia friends had been following the case since indictment, and no matter the skill he brought to the table, they considered the case to be an inevitable loser.

Do you ever get tired of other people's eternal pessimism or dejection? Stanley did. More than once he would find an associate in the library the night before his or her trial with head down and files everywhere, certain the opposition would have a field day the following morning. Stanley would more than likely offer the following thought to these younger lawyers, but it transcends the law and is universal: "Anyone can lose a case – it takes thought, work, and creativity to win them." This must have been on his mind as he accepted the Wecht representation.

The media wasn't skeptical for long. Pittsburgh's city papers provided an almost blow by blow description of the trial. Journalists were discovering, and writing about, Stanley's legendary command of the court. The Pittsburgh Post-Gazette published an op-ed piece by staff writer James O'Toole entitled "Wecht's Lawyer is the Star of the Courtroom." "The arguments are tedious, and discussions of surgical slides make for indifferent drama. But Preiser gives the proceedings a lift. He brings the ABC's – Arrogance, Brilliance, and Confidence into the service of his client," wrote columnist Roy McHugh. When all was said and done, more than one member of the jury made sure to seek out Stanley for an autograph.

Stanley obliterated the prosecutor's case. He showed the jury the high level of service Dr. Wecht's private lab often donated to the county. He demonstrated the large number of vital forensic determinations the lab had provided to Allegheny county free of charge. He explained how the county lab and its employees received training under Dr. Wecht they were unlikely to get anywhere else. And he brought the evidence to show how certain people were out to get Cyril's job.

The jury acquitted on all counts.

Justice had indeed been served for Dr. Wecht and the people of Pittsburgh, and the verdict was heard loud and clear across the country. Stanley was more in demand than ever, but this case wasn't over. Stanley's friend and client had been maligned.

During the lead up to the trial, Allegheny County Commissioner Jack Lynch had called in to a radio show and announced that, "Cyril Wecht is no doctor at all." On behalf of Dr. Wecht, Stanley sued Lynch, alleging that Lynch had defamed Dr. Wecht's character and professional abilities. Lynch hired Bob Potter, an excellent attorney, to defend him. Potter later described the following scene to Pittsburgh attorney Gregg Rosen, who related it to me.

Stanley and the stenographer were, as always, early, and were waiting in a conference room when Lynch and Potter arrived. Stanley skipped the usual pleasantries and went right to work. Most lawyers begin a deposition with softball questions to a witness about name, occupation, etc. Not Stanley Preiser. With his back to Lynch and Bob, Stanley growled, "Swear the witness." Once sworn, Stanley abruptly swiveled in his chair to confront Lynch. He glared at Lynch and again growled, "Wecht is no doctor at all. Did you say that?" Everyone from Pennsylvania to California knew Cyril Wecht was a medical doctor. Lynch hung his head and admitted both that he made the statement, and that it was false.

According to Potter, thru Rosen, Lynch never recovered from the opening question. Stanley savaged him throughout the deposition. Soon afterwards, the case was settled, and Lynch took to the airways once more, this time to issue a profuse public apology for defaming Dr. Wecht.

In the winter of 1981, Stanley created a new trial practice course for the Nova University Law Center in Ft. Lauderdale. Classes were three hours every Monday night for a little over two months. Stanley taught each week, and he brought guest speakers such as Mel Belli, Harry Philo (ATLA President), Richard Neely (Chief Justice of the West Virginia Supreme Court), Lee Bailey, and others.

The school paper, in an editorial, wrote: "Congratulations to the Administration and Faculty of the Law Center for providing a unique and outstanding alternative course – Trial Tactics and Strategy taught by Stanley Preiser. We urge the Administration to make this a permanent part of the curriculum." Unfortunately, other matters would keep Stanley from teaching the course again.

In 1982, the episode Stanley had expected much earlier finally came to pass. At only 55 years of age he suffered a severe heart attack. The 30+ years of cigarettes, cigars and pipes; the all-nighters; the alcohol; the diet; and the stress all ganged up on his heart at one time. Dad never feared death – only incapacitation. We were all under strict instructions that no heroic intervention was to be given if he was not going to substantially recuperate.

We were told he died twice that night at the hospital, only to be shocked back to life, and open- heart surgery (still in relative infancy 38 years ago) was performed to replace a valve as soon as possible. Some of the heart tissue had been destroyed. But for his constitution and the fact he had quit smoking ten years before, the doctors said he would not have survived.

None of his family or colleagues had ever seen Stanley quite so despondent in the early days following surgery. As much as he loved his wife, son, daughter, and daughter-in-law, I'm not certain that would have been enough to pull him through. But there was a new family member – Sara's and my daughter Blair, who was by then about a year and a half. She had Stanley enthralled since she was a month or two old. Sara and I reminded him that we were new to the parenting game and asked what might happen to Blair if he was not there to take care of her? Did he not want to see her Bat Mitzvah, college graduation, and maybe even marriage? Well, we can't know if it is true, and some may ascribe other reasons for Dad's sudden alertness and determination to return to normalcy, but his family is convinced he would not leave Blair.

They were close almost from her birth, and that love lasted until his death twenty-seven years later and, according to Blair, even beyond. He did, by the way, dance at her Bat Mitzvah, celebrate her graduation from college, and took great pride in her becoming a Pittsburgh lawyer. And again, while we can't know if it's true, his family is convinced he was popping heavenly Champagne like a pro with the rest of us at both of his grandchildren's weddings.

Back to 1982. While Stanley recovered, the business of the firm on behalf of its clients had to continue. Don was now first in command. We had excellent lawyers, and the firm functioned fine while Stanley recuperated. Not surprisingly, once he made up his mind to get well, he did so in Stanley fashion – on his own terms and fast. Within a month he was working from, and holding meetings at, his home. Don was invaluable at the office, as well as substituting for Stanley at meetings, before certain judges, and serving as the face of the firm.

I had been assisting Stanley on a major pharmaceutical product liability case to be tried in Fairmont, WV, in early 1982. Don took over and I had the opportunity to assist (and I do mean assist) and observe an artist. Our client was taking the blood thinner Coumadin and had suffered a hemorrhagic infarction, which killed skin and muscle on her thigh from bone to surface. The jury found that the manufacturer had failed to warn of the specifics and the seriousness of what might happen if certain blood clotting tests were not performed as recommended. The award was the largest in Marion County history, and the manufacturer later modified the warning so no one else would go through the hell suffered by our client.

On the three-hour drive home Don was in a pretty good mood. He told me a number of stories about his life, including one particularly bawdy tale about a girl in New Orleans. In the middle of the story he stopped, looked at me, and said, "You know, that never happened. As I get older, I seem to tell stories that I have convinced myself are true, but often they are not." I loved Don Wilson. His untimely death a year later at only 66 was hard for us all.

Within six months or so Stanley was back at the helm. He was also in good shape. He and Joyce had discovered the Pritikin Longevity Center in Miami Beach. They loved the Center's mantra of balanced living, properly performed exercise, and foods with manageable salt and fat content. Stanley credited Pritikin with keeping him healthy for another 20+ years.

Lest there be any doubt that Stanley felt close to 100%, in October of 1982 he began to prepare for another Pittsburgh trial. He was defending a relatively shady character named Thomas Skelton, who had been charged with paying $10,000 to have a man killed. Barbara Fleisher, now a seasoned criminal lawyer, was an excellent second chair in a case with overtones of danger.

The witnesses against Skelton were three racketeers who had flipped to testify they heard Skelton put out the contract. They had, in other words, made deals with the government concerning their own crimes in exchange for their testimony against Skelton. Stanley's strategy was to discredit these men to such an extent that no defense would have to be offered. He employed two jury selection experts and spent three weeks picking the jury. His plan worked. Once he was finished dismantling the testimony of the three supposed eye witnesses, he rested his case, relying only on his previous cross examination and upcoming closing argument. The jury quickly returned with a "Not Guilty" verdict.

This case was mentioned in the book, *Pittsburgh Characters*, in one of the chapters written by Paul Maryniak:

Skelton engaged West Virginia's version of Perry Mason, Stanley Preiser, who earlier had presented a brilliant defense of former Allegheny County coroner and commissioner Cyril Wecht on fraud charges. [The prosecution and its witnesses] were no match for the quick-witted Preiser, who resembled a boxer in an elegant pin-stripe suit. As tenacious as he was eloquent . . ., he proceeded to cast aspersions on every statement that fell from the disreputable informants' lips. With his aw-shucks Southern accent and down-home demeanor, Preiser sweet talked the jury into acquitting Skelton.

I was not at this trial, but happened to arrive in Pittsburgh on another matter the afternoon of the acquittal. I went to the hotel where Stanley and Barbara were staying, and found that Skelton had reserved the entire floor. He had armed friends guarding the elevators and checking visitors, and every bottle of Champagne the hotel could locate in Pittsburgh had been brought over for the celebratory crowd's enjoyment. It was some party. I hope Mr. Skelton enjoyed it, because within the year he mysteriously disappeared, and no one ever heard from him again.

Based on Stanley's aggressive courtroom tactics, one might think he had a strained relationship with opposing counsel all the time, but this isn't so. In fact, he relished a bright opponent, and respected them as long as they were honorable. Gregg Rosen says he referred cases to Stanley when he needed to prove night was day and day was night. He described Stanley's relationships with lawyers who lost cases to him in this way:

Stanley was mostly magnanimous toward his defeated legal adversaries. He would routinely praise them as great lawyers.

Imagine the effect on the defeated lawyer. Yes, he could tell his friends, it is true that he lost his case to Stanley Preiser, but he was a great lawyer defeated by another great lawyer. Stanley had said so himself. How much greater Stanley's compliments also made him in the subsequent telling of the tale by the defeated lawyer.

On one occasion, I was walking with Stanley when we encountered an old law school classmate of mine, Sumner. He was a former Marine sergeant and journeyman criminal defense lawyer who depended on court appointments to represent indigents to make a living. I introduced my friend to Stanley, and Sumner immediately stood at attention in recognition of Stanley's reputation. When I told Stanley my friend's name, Stanley immediately said, "I have heard of you Sumner, people say great things about you." Of course, Stanley had never heard anything about my friend, but my friend ate it up. I am sure he has spent the rest of his life bragging to his friends that the great Stanley Preiser had heard of him. Stanley was sufficiently self-confident that he could afford to praise his enemies and other lesser lawyers.

By this time, and even a bit earlier, our litigators' reach had indeed expanded across the county, both in the medical negligence field, as well as a new arena that would not only take us world-wide, but have a vital impact on the life of the nation's children.

In 1975, eight-month-old Kelli Holcomb received her first DPT (Diphtheria, Pertussis [whooping cough], Tetanus) inoculation in West Virginia. She screamed inconsolably for over an hour, had a small seizure, and spiked a fever of over 103 degrees. By the next day, all seemed well. A few months later Kelli received her next prescribed DPT shot. Within 48 hours she had developed permanent paralysis in both legs, as well as seizures.

Kelli's father approached Stanley in 1981 with questions about whether the vaccine could have caused his daughter's damage, and whether there was any recourse. Kelli, now a beautiful six-year-old, was growing and needed wheel chairs, medications, special beds, modifications to the home, physical therapies, full time aides to care for and lift her, and much more.

We discovered in our initial research that there had been only a few cases involving injuries allegedly caused by a poorly manufactured DPT vaccine. Plaintiffs' had also alleged the failure of pediatricians to be as aware as they should be of signs that were contraindications to the second or third round of the generally recommended shots. None of these claims had been successful.

Stanley asked William Druckman, Dr./Lawyer Richard Lindsay, and me to spearhead the investigation into the vaccine and keep him well informed. The expense of investigation would be enormous, but the payoff in the form of a potentially safer vaccine, better informed physicians, and substantial legal fees, was deemed worth the risk.

After exhaustive research and meetings with experts, we discovered two very important facts. First, there had been articles published in medical journals that advised against giving a second DPT shot if the patient had reacted badly to the first. Second, there seemed to be many more serious reactions to the DPT vaccine than was generally known.

Stanley always said that the greatest investigator in the world is the smart trial lawyer with an expert and a subpoena. And we were not going to learn much more without filing a lawsuit. Stanley devised a strategy, pored over the opinions and qualifications of the expert witnesses that Druckman, Lindsay, and I had interviewed, and filed a Complaint in the Southern District of West Virginia against a single defendant, Richardson-Merrill, the Cincinnati based manufacturer of the DPT vaccine. Unfortunately, the pediatrician who gave Kelly her first and follow-up shot was deceased and there was no viable estate to sue.

Once suit was commenced, we were entitled to discovery. This meant we could depose all of the people involved in manufacturing and promoting this vaccine. We could, and would, search through and review hundreds of thousands of pages documenting their research, internal communications, actions, knowledge of DPT reactions, and, vitally, their inactions. The search for documents at the Defendant's headquarters alone took days. The pharmaceutical house had brought in a dozen lawyers who obstructed our efforts all they could, which led to us obtaining a court order instructing Merrill's lawyers to provide us with a private, comfortable room. They could sit outside to be sure we stole no documents, but otherwise they were to leave us alone. If we wanted copies, we were to mark them, and the company's lawyers were to provide them.

An entire book could be written about the Holcomb case and the litigation that followed, but I'll synopsize it the best I can. We learned that about 1 in every 100,000 children born in the U.S. suffered some sort of permanent damage from the vaccine to their central nervous system (brain and spinal cord). That is a staggering number when you know that every infant receives three doses. We learned that it was the Pertussis component of the triple shot that was the culprit. No one yet knew exactly why, but the strict liability laws that been established gave us a chance even if we could not identify the precise pathogenesis.

We discovered that there were articles written by respected doctors warning against a second or third shot if the pediatrician had been told about the symptoms shown by Kelli after her first dose. However, these warnings were not contained in the material distributed with the vaccine to doctors by Merrill.

The company took the position that there was no real proof that the vaccine caused the injury. According to the defense, Merrill did the best job they could during the manufacturing process, the vaccine was within industry standards since other companies manufactured it in the same manner, and the Government had given approval. Also, any conclusion that the vaccine caused injury was just that, a supposition based solely on the proximity of time between the shot and the development of symptoms. No medical test proved the cause of any injury – it was simply coincidental to the time of the inoculation. These were formidable defenses at the time.

We, on the other hand, contended that Richardson-Merrill had distributed a product about which they had received reports of its suspected dangers, and did nothing about it. We also argued that the company had the duty to properly warn physicians about the risks and warning signs that should prevent further vaccinations, yet the company had breached that duty to horrific ends.

As I alluded to above, Bill, Richard, and I had performed the leg work under Stanley's direction, and then Stanley wove the evidence together like a skilled artisan. At the pre-trial settlement conference, he was masterful, and the result was a $690,000 (about 1.85 million in 2020 dollars) settlement, the first-ever payment for a DPT injury by a vaccine's manufacturer.

Within two weeks, Danny Smith's parents saw an article about the Holcomb case in a tabloid in Maryland, contacted a local attorney, and that lawyer contacted us. Danny's story was similar to Kelli's, except he suffered from transverse myelitis, an inflammation of both sides of part of his spinal cord that prevented him from walking.

It would be in this early case that we discovered something in the manufacturer's files that I don't believe was in Merrill's. Eli Lilly, a major pharmaceutical company, had written an in-house memo deeming it necessary to clean the nucleus of the Pertussis component of the vaccine to avoid harm. We would later discover that all other subsequent defendant pharmaceutical houses had a copy of this Lilly memo in their files as well. And we learned that none of the manufacturers, including the one in Danny's case, had taken the precautions set forth by Lilly.

Was the memo simply discounted, or did these manufacturers believe it would never see the light of day? Either way, this "smoking gun" was now out there, and was damning.

Unlike Kelli's doctor, who had died before we entered the case, Danny's doctor was still practicing. Accordingly, we sued the manufacturer and the pediatrician who had administered subsequent doses after Danny had reacted badly to the first shot. We alleged that even if the manufacturer had failed to warn physicians about the contraindications, the doctors still had a duty to read the literature and know about the adverse, though temporary, reactions to the first shot contraindicating the damaging second. This time, both the manufacturer and doctor contributed to the successful settlement of a very large, but confidential, amount.

As often happens after a product has been successfully shown to be dangerous, scores of possible cases began cropping up. Because we had received a great deal of national exposure for winning the first case, and given that most other lawyers did not want to "reinvent the wheel," we were receiving a great many referrals.

For the next four to five years, our firm expended hundreds of thousands of hours and dollars representing many babies injured by the DPT vaccine. Besides West Virginia, we won cases in North Carolina, Idaho, New York, Texas, Pennsylvania, California,

Maryland, Virginia, Kentucky, Ohio, and Washington D.C. I primarily took care of the malpractice litigation against the doctors, while some of my colleagues concentrated on the cases against the manufacturers. Credit goes to them for finally getting the attention of Big Pharma with significant jury verdicts when the cases failed to settle.

Other firms around the country also began to specialize in DPT litigation after we established a pattern of wins and shared our knowledge at legal symposia. By then there were four or five other manufacturers identified, all using the same poor process as Merrill despite having the Lilly memo. Further, there were still many doctors not keeping up with relevant articles in their field.

As every seasoned product liability lawyer knows, manufacturers usually refuse to make changes to a defective product until the verdicts and settlements encroach significantly on their profits. Finally, then, in the late 1980's the industry corrected the Pertussis formula, and changed the warnings so they were properly written, displayed, and instructive. It is likely that hundreds of thousands of children have since been spared lives of great difficulty because of these cases. Though many outstanding lawyers around the nation were ultimately part of the heroic effort to make this so, the genesis can be traced back to Stanley Preiser's decision to accept that first case in hopes of protecting the public, as well as the investigation performed by Bill Druckman, Richard Lindsay, and, I hope to some degree, me.

As of 2020, the rate of reaction to the DPT vaccine is very low. My son did not receive the Pertussis portion of the shot in 1982, but I did not object to the present DPT vaccine being administered to my grandchildren over the last decade.

Enhancements to the length and quality of life often follow abatement of stress. A major change took place in 1983 which had such an impact on Stanley's life. For a number of years, Stanley had been representing one of the country's wealthiest men, Thomas Worrell of Charlottesville, VA, in both his personal domestic matters, and litigation involving Worrell's chain of newspapers. Stanley and Tom, who also held a law degree, became as close as good friends can be – they were like brothers.

Stanley's hard driving lifestyle had already taken its toll in the form of one heart attack, and even after he began to attend Pritikin on a somewhat regular basis, there were concerns about the strength of his heart and his blood pressure. The firm had grown to such a size, and was handling so many contingency fee cases, that on any given day Stanley might have a million dollars or more (which, it is hard to believe, is close to five million in 2020 dollars) tied up in case expenses. One can easily understand the constant stress a sole owner would experience in that situation.

It was not in Stanley's personality to let anyone know he was ever ill. To the world he was again strong and fit, but his family, close friends, and doctors were aware of the hypertension and heart involvement, and they were worried about him.

Ultra-wealthy Tom Worrell was someone who was not only concerned, but had the means to do something about it. Tom was a great friend and an equally astute businessman who saw an opportunity. He reasoned that if Stanley were able to run the law firm without the financial pressure, he could stay healthier, handle more cases, and bring in more income. In effect, Tom Worrell became an investor in the firm, which the law permitted since he was an attorney.

Thus, Preiser and Wilson Legal Corporation was formed. The directors and officers were Stanley and a few trusted attorneys who worked for Worrell. Tom reimbursed Stanley for all outstanding expenses and became responsible for all future monetary advances and salaries. He had found a way to help everyone make some money while simultaneously relieving much of the pressure affecting his friend's health. Preiser and Wilson would look and operate essentially the same as ever, but this change indeed made life easier for Stanley, and also came with numerous substantial individual perks, including an Excalibur.

Stanley had a client in 1983 who alleged he had been damaged when a soda bottle blew up and a piece of glass cut his Achilles tendon. Fortunately for the client, he had healed pretty well. There was a one-day trial and the defense argued that a soda bottle could not simply blow up without the plaintiff abusing the bottle in some manner. The defense lawyer had a six-pack of the same soda bottles at his counsel table. In a seemingly miraculous stroke of luck for the plaintiff and Lady Justice, as the defense lawyer was finishing his closing argument, one of the bottles on his table, sitting alone and without abuse, exploded.

Stanley believed in luck as a concept, but mostly as it related to how the cards were first dealt. He played a lot of cards, but only games that after the deal involved skill (such as Bridge, Poker, or Gin) and never of pure chance (Baccarat). He also loved other games of skill, such as Craps (he was a semi-legend at trial lawyers' meetings where crowds would gather to watch him play), but never "come-ons" such as Roulette or Slots. This philosophy easily transitioned into his feeling about trying cases and living life in general. He was sure that: "Luck is a loser's excuse for a winner's effort and commitment."

Fortunately, no one was harmed this time by the exploding bottle, but the judge and Stanley were doing all they could not to break out laughing. The judge had the jury escorted out of the courtroom, and once they were gone, the laughter really came out. At this point, defense counsel requested a mis-trial, which only made the judge laugh harder. Needless to say, the case was over without having to call the jury back. Stanley's only quip? "I would rather be lucky than good."

Stanley and Joyce decided to start taking it a bit easier. In late 1983, they bought a condominium in Boca Raton, where they began to spend much of the winter. Around this same time, the ten lawyers who made up Preiser and Wilson bought the business from Tom Worrell and became equal partners, while Stanley became "Of Counsel." The firm retained the name Preiser and Wilson. Stanley was still an important part of the equation in terms of attracting business, offering advice, and handling cases.

In 1984, the tobacco industry was already under fire for the vast array of damages caused by its products. Cases had been filed and lawyers were beginning to specialize in going after Big Tobacco. Stanley felt that the lawyers bringing these suits were missing an important allegation, and ultimately brought the first suit against the tobacco industry contending that the warnings the producers used were inadequate because they failed to address the addictive qualities of nicotine.

The firm was seriously busy with its DPT and other litigation at the time. We had established a niche for pharmaceutical cases of all types, and lawyers from around the country were sending them our way. We decided to do the same with the tobacco suit in reverse, and referred it to a group of lawyers who had developed their own niche handling that type litigation. As we now know, the lawyers at the top of the chain in the tobacco cases ultimately justly earned gazillions, but it took a toll on many of them. I think Stanley and the firm made the right decision to pass.

Gregg Rosen backed up his claim that Stanley could turn night to day and vice versa with this entertaining story about another

Pittsburgh case he referred to Stanley:

We had a case against a life insurer who refused to pay a $1 million life insurance policy by claiming fraud in the application process. The insurer claimed that our client lied in the life insurance application when he answered "no" to two questions: "Have you ever drank alcohol to excess or intoxication?" and "Have you ever been diagnosed with a disease or disorder of the liver?" In fact, the record seemed clear otherwise. The doctor's notes had my client admitting he drank a fifth of whiskey per day for 25 years and that he had cirrhosis of the liver (diagnosed by his surgeon on visual inspection during gall bladder surgery). Shortly before the deposition, on a lark, Stanley called for the Oxford English Dictionary definition of "intoxication."

The dictionary's example of intoxication was a person imagining wood nymphs gallivanting around a forest. We had the dictionary on the conference room table at the start of the session. Stanley began the deposition of the insurance company's claim's manager with the insurer's denial letter, which explained that the insured lied by denying he drank to intoxication. "Mr. Dieterich," Stanley asked, "Can you define 'intoxication?'" Dieterich fumbled around and finally admitted he could not define the term. We showed Dieterich the dictionary. Then Stanley asked, "Mr. Dieterich, when you wrote this letter, did you believe that my client actually drank to the point that he imagined wood nymphs gallivanting around a forest?" "No", Dieterich admitted. Dieterich's deposition proceeded downhill for him from there.

In the same case, Stanley prepared the surgeon, whose post op notes described our client's liver as cirrhotic. It was as though Stanley was a snake charmer, and he hypnotized this doctor.

When the depo prep was complete, the surgeon assured us that our client did not have a cirrhotic liver. At his ensuing deposition called by the insurance company, the surgeon clung fast to the position Stanley had charmed into him. "Yes, my notes say that, but the patient's liver was not cirrhotic." "Yes, my notes say that, but I did not mean what my notes say." On and on. The insurer's lawyer was apoplectic and disbelievingly waving the post op notes around. We settled that case on very favorable terms - another example of Stanley proving that night was day and white was black.

Stanley hated bullies. One such person called Stanley's bookkeeper and friend a "bitch," and Stanley sued him under the insulting words statute. He obtained a verdict for $195,000. Everyone knew the courts would not let that verdict stand. It was far too much money for an instance where a jerk simply called someone a name. However, it had very satisfying for both client and lawyer as the animal got slaughtered, so to speak.

Bill Druckman worked on the appeal in that case and recalls:

At some point I volunteered to help write the appellate brief. Stanley was getting ready for a trial and had laryngitis. So, when I gave him the first draft of the brief, he couldn't yell at me. Instead, he used a legal pad and wrote, "This brief is Shit, Shit, Shit!" One of the lawyers in the firm who had just won a nice verdict walked by, and Stanley wrote congratulations on the legal pad for him, and then continued destroying me in large scribbled letters. Finally, I got the brief to where it passed Stanley's inspection, but, as predicted, the court reversed on technical grounds, and then the case settled for very little. Still, the client was very happy, and the bully never bothered her again.

1985 brought with it another Pittsburgh case for Stanley and Barbara – one that yielded more than its share of anecdotal material. Well-known businessman Elmer Jonnet had been convicted of perjury in a federal trial the year before, but the verdict was set aside by the appellate court and sent back to the lower court for retrial. Stanley was engaged by Jonnet at the behest of Jonnet's personal counsel Gregg Rosen and his partner George Mahfood, the latter being as versatile and bright as Gregg. They had been working with Stanley on cases since 1982, and made it clear to Elmer they thought Stanley was one of the best.

The same judge who heard the first trial, District Judge Hubert Teitelbaum, would hear the second. By then, Stanley was sort of a celebrity in Pittsburgh, and, for whatever reason, Teitelbaum simply did not like him. According to Stanley, not only was the judge nasty to him, but he was condescending to Barbara. Stanley, being Stanley, "called" the judge on it, and was rewarded with some very harsh and inappropriate words. As Stanley delved deeper into the case, he turned up some pretty good evidence that Teitelbaum didn't like Jonnet either. The judge had denied Jonnet bail, strangely keeping him in jail on a perjury charge (we aren't talking murder, after all), imposed the maximum sentence possible, sent Elmer immediately to prison, and threatened to hold his first lawyer in contempt. The word "meshuggah" comes to mind.

And then came the first coup de grace. Stanley asked the judge to schedule the case so those who were Jewish could observe the Jewish High Holy Days. In response, the judge called Stanley a "dumb Jew." This prompted a retort from George Mahfood, "Stanley, I didn't know you were Jewish – I've never met a dumb Jew before."

Stanley then filed a motion asking Teitelbaum to recuse himself from the case for all the above reasons. Teitelbaum denied that motion, but it became apparent that the appellate court was going to remove him anyway. In the face of that removal, he stepped down, but not before issuing a statement that he did so "because of the reprehensible accusations made by Preiser to discredit me." A new judge was assigned and the trial went forward.

George Mahfood relates an improbable event that occurred toward the end of the prosecution's case:

> *In the retrial, the government offered the testimony of the FBI's chief document examiner to testify that the relevant contract in the underlying case which Elmer testified was authentic, was actually an altered document. Stanley's review of this examiner's file revealed that the government had repeatedly rejected his opinions as insufficient, so the government sent the expert a copy of the report prepared by Jonnet's opposition's expert in the civil case in order to bolster the FBI's report. On cross-examination, Stanley literally reduced the FBI's chief document examiner to a physically shaking, incredibly incompetent witness. The government's entire case was destroyed in one afternoon.*
>
> *Then something happened that I had never seen before and will never see again. At the conclusion of his testimony, the FBI's witness asked the trial judge if he could take his file with him. The trial judge asked counsel if they had any objection. Stanley said, with a touch of disgust, "Your honor, the witness can take his file and leave." As Stanley said this, he gestured with his fist and his thumb in the manner of a baseball umpire signaling a runner out at home plate. At that moment, two jurors looked at the witness, and, mimicking Stanley, thumbed the witness out of there, too.*

Following what was obviously the fall of the case for the prosecution, the judge asked all counsel to meet him in chambers. Stanley came out and informed Elmer that the Government had offered to reduce the charge to a minor misdemeanor if Elmer took a deal. Elmer would be sentenced to time already spent in jail, and they could all go home. After Stanley recommended the deal, Elmer asked Gregg Rosen for his opinion on what he should do. Gregg told him to listen to Stanley. But Elmer was tough. He said that Stanley was the greatest lawyer and showman he had ever seen, and he wanted to roll the dice with the jury.

The trial went on. Stanley had waived his opening statement until after the prosecution finished laying out its case, and delivered it at this time. He then rested without calling witnesses and immediately was allowed to begin his summation. Elmer turned out to be prescient. He was acquitted by the jury on all counts.

Stanley later filed a complaint against Teitelbaum before the Judicial Ethics Board. The results were not publicized, but I could tell from Dad's face that some sort of discipline was meted out.

Interestingly, three years later Teitelbaum faced further charges of bias and misconduct after he threatened to hold a female lawyer in contempt if she used her maiden name instead of her husband's name. For that one, the appellate court stripped him of all his cases for a while.

Notwithstanding the Teitelbaum episode, Stanley had amazing rapport with most judges, doctors, and public officials. It often allowed him great latitude. A trial in northern West Virginia before a newly elected judge comes to mind. Stanley had a twenty-year friendship with the judge at the time he took the bench, yet from that day forward Stanley always called him "Judge," even in casual settings and/or when alone. There are two shining examples of how this philosophy played out well for him, and might for most.

In the first case, during trial the mother of a deceased teenager was not showing the needed emotion under Stanley's direct examination. Stanley suddenly stopped, walked behind the judge's bench to his private bathroom, and began to sniff and cry, as if the moment had gotten to him (maybe it had). The judge just sat there. A minute or two later Stanley emerged. By then the mother, and most of the jury, were in tears, so Stanley just sat down. The judge called a recess and defense counsel, one of the best, came over to Stanley and asked him what he needed to settle. This kind of patience on the part of a jurist is almost unheard of. Here, however, Stanley was a favorite, and I am quite convinced his deference to the judge as far as his title allowed him to get away with what some might call a little shenanigan.

The next experience was described by attorney John Romano, who you will hear more about:

> *There was a time in the mid 1980's when our law firm was handling cases in the Dalkon Shield Litigation. Former federal Judge Robert Merhige, Jr. out of Richmond, Virginia, had just entered a "Stay" in all litigation relating to Dalkon Shield IUD's because the A.H. Robins Co. as the manufacturer had just filed for bankruptcy protection. Many plaintiffs' lawyers, including myself and one of my partners, concluded that the Stay only applied to the A.H. Robins Co. as a defendant and that if there were other defendants in the case, we could continue to proceed against them — i.e. taking depositions, etc. So, we continued to try and move the case forward against these other defendants.*

> *One morning, there was a knock at our door and it was a Federal Marshal — who at the time appeared to me to be about*

*10-feet tall and mean as hell and with a crazy grin on his face –
and he handed me a "Show Cause Order" from Judge Merhige,
Jr. As it turns out, the Judge concluded that those lawyers who
continued to proceed with activities in such cases as ours were
in violation of his Order. We were served on a Thursday with
an Order to be in his Court Monday morning at 9:00 a.m. in
Richmond, Virginia. I told my partner we need representation
because, as the saying goes, "Only a fool has himself for a lawyer."*

*We, of course, turned immediately to Stanley Preiser. He
worked with us the entire weekend. Stanley accompanied Mike
Eriksen and me to Richmond that Sunday and we appeared
Monday morning in front of Judge Merhige. Amazingly, our
case was the first case called. Also – and even more amazingly
– the Judge basically gave about a 10-minute presentation to everyone in the courtroom – and it was about Stanley Preiser. I had
been unaware of the fact that Stanley had appeared many times
in front of Judge Merhige. I was also unaware that the Judge
considered Stanley Preiser – as the Judge said that morning – to
be the single greatest lawyer "in America today." It was an unusual situation, as our hearing took place before the main hearing,
and Judge Merhige simply wanted us to apologize and not do it
again. The hearing was over before we knew it – but the Judge
had let everyone in that Court on that day know his opinion of
Stanley Preiser.*

The bottom line is pure Stanley: "There is nothing people like
more than hearing their own name and title out loud. You always
want to make your friends and acquaintance feel good, and it will
usually come back around to help you, too."

After the Jonnet trial, Stanley and Joyce moved to Florida full time and became residents of the Sunshine State. This did not mean in any way that he was going to stop practicing, but after 35 years of trying probably as many major cases as any lawyer alive, he was ready to move down a different path. He became "Of Counsel" to two of the recognized top firms in the area – a corporate firm building a trial practice in Boca Raton, and the best trial firm in Palm Beach County - John Romano's.

About a year later in 1986, I left Preiser and Wilson and the firm had to drop the Preiser name. Just as with an anthropological tree where at some time in history one species goes one way and one another, that is how the balance of this biography, which is about Stanley, will treat my launching my own firm with Stanley as co-counsel. We went one way and the other branch/old firm went another way and had little impact on Stanley's life thereafter. The Preiser and Wilson chapter was essentially closed.

ROUND FIFTEEN
(the last round)
1987 – 2009

Stanley and Joyce enjoyed their condominium in Boca Raton, but once they moved into it full time, it wasn't long before the close quarters began suggesting the need for a new house. They purchased a large home in the Boca Grove Country Club Community, one of the premiere gated developments in the growing city.

This type of South Florida country club living proved to be perfect for both Stanley and Joyce. They were in their late 50's – relative youngsters to most of Florida's retirees. The house sat on a golf course, and for the first time in 13 years, they had time to really take up the game. They enjoyed the Club's lounge and restaurant four or five nights a week. Joyce played cards or Mahjong twice a week, and they frequently entertained, or were entertained by, their many friends. They took advantage of the warm weather, relished time together grilling and relaxing at their pool, and replaced the often-relentless ringing of the phone with their favorite music. They became so social that when Sara and I moved to Boca Raton in 1992, even *we* had a tough time finding a free slot in their social calendar.

It seemed to Stanley that the natural next step for a full-time Floridian was to buy his own boat. He purchased a small walkabout for parties and fishing, and named it the *Joy-Sea*, after his beloved "Joycie." He even commissioned long-sleeved red shirts with the boat's name on them for the family to wear.

Stanley often had a lot on his mind, and riding with him in a car had brought many people to prayer over the years. He quickly established that he had similar nautical "talents," taking out a good part of the wooden dock as he backed out at the start of a particularly memorable early morning excursion. From then on, discretion being the better part of valor, he hosted his family, which now included two toddler-aged grandchildren, either while tethered to the dock or at sea with a certified captain.

In reference to home ownership, Stanley often quipped, "A house is a thief, but you have to pay the ransom because it's usually one's largest asset." When the *Joy-Sea* began showing similar extortionist tendencies after about two years, Stanley decided it was time to let her go. He loved entertaining on that boat, but as almost any ex-boat owner will predict, Stanley's best day with the vessel was the day she became someone else's problem.

In the mid 1990's, my sister Terri, also living in Boca Raton, decided to install a lap pool at her home. Fred Delp came to lay out the design for the project, and they started talking. Fred was an interesting guy to be sure. Coincidentally, he had been born in a small town in West Virginia, and said he had spent much of his childhood carrying his polio-stricken younger brother around on his back. Fred loved sports, was an avid fisherman, and a hard worker. He and Terri hit it off.

Fred was also a good (not great, mind you) guitarist. Terri played a little piano and had dabbled in some song writing in the past. Not long after they met, a spectacular idea took wing. They found a niche and began co-writing and performing songs about fishing and children's safety. The songs did not have to rival Gershwin or Swift to be successful - they had to be, *and many were*, cute, catchy, and have relatable standard melodies with clever lyrics. My personal favorite was called *Do Fish Get a Tan*, where the lyrics ask:

> *What happens on a rainy day?*
> *Do fish have umbrellas that work the other way?*
> *And on a sunny day, do fish get a tan?*
> *Do they talk to each other about catchin' a man?*

The safety songs were perfect to help small children learn and remember concepts like knowing their address and phone number, having an emergency fire safety plan, and understanding that "dangerous strangers" do not always come in the form of scary men.

To a great degree because he wanted to, rather than because superior talent was being demonstrated, Stanley envisioned a successful music business in the making. He staked Terri with enough funds to start *Fishbone Fred Enterprises*. Not too long after, Terri and Fred got married (each for the third time) and began entertaining in public based on their music. While they weren't making enough to pay Stanley back, they were more or less covering their expenses.

Whether Terri and Fred were good enough to ever move into a broader, more visible, musical strata is a matter of opinion, but Stanley wanted to turn Fred into a TV and Las Vegas-type star. Stanley may not have had the best musical ear, but he encouraged Terri to pursue the venture. As he had demonstrated with the horses, he wanted her to live her life in a way that would make her happy and fulfilled, and he was in a position to help. He called a meeting of his closest friends and relatives, and we all became investors in *Fishbone Fred*.

Stanley invested perhaps 5 times more money than the rest of us put together, and gave Terri and Fred the go ahead to do what was necessary to take the next step forward. Stanley, himself, was looking forward to this endeavor as well. He used his Las Vegas contacts to set up audition shows with dancers, beautiful show girls, etc. at casino hotels in Las Vegas and Biloxi, Mississippi. He also engaged agents to put together a *Fishbone Fred* television show for kids, which even completed a few pilot episodes.

Unfortunately, no matter how hard Dad, Fred, and Terri tried, it became apparent that the chances of *Fishbone Fred* hitting it big singing American standards, rock, and country, were pretty non-existent. *Fishbone Fred* never became the sensation they had hoped. Some thought they should return to the fishing/safety niche they had established, but they never did. Stanley allowed Fred and Terri to push on for a few more years until they ultimately divorced around 2012. And just as with the horses, Stanley (and this time all of the investors) lost a lot of money. I think Dad enjoyed the glitz and the challenge with *Fishbone* more than he did the horse business, but neither raised his tax payments, that's for certain.

Enjoying life in the sun did not keep Stanley from continuing to work in West Virginia, Florida, Pennsylvania, and Virginia. His growing representation of Tom Worrell's empire put both prop and jet aircraft at his disposal, and made travel easy and quick. After 1987, and up until about 1997, he also served as "Of Counsel" to my law firm, which now had offices in Charleston, Pittsburgh, and Boca Raton, and he worked out of those offices when he desired.

Various publishers had been asking Stanley for many years to revise, republish, and modernize his best-selling book of 1966 about neck and back sprain cases. Stanley's name was so well known by now in the legal community that the publishers assumed whatever he wrote would be a smash.

Not surprisingly, it had been a number of years since he had tried a simple neck and back sprain case. However, major injury cases often involved damage to soft tissue. In 1987, Stanley, Cyril Wecht, and I set out to write the three-volume series, *Handling Soft Tissue Injury Cases*.

While the general concept of persuasion had not changed, there were many updated areas to cover after twenty years. For example, diagnostic techniques available by the 1980's, like CT scans and early MRIs, gave plaintiffs objective evidence of soft tissue damage that a flat x-ray simply could not provide. Defense lawyers could no longer put medical experts on the stand to mislead the jury with an x-ray that "didn't show" an injury. Advances in computer technology, and particularly computer simulations, also provided improved methods of presenting evidence, and modern times offered a much more sophisticated cadre of experts from which to choose (biomechanical engineers, for example).

The first volume consisted primarily of trial strategies. The second two volumes were written primarily by Dr. Wecht, and covered soft tissue involvement in almost every medical discipline. The series was such a success that 2 years later, in 1989, the three of us published another three-volume series entitled *Preparing and Winning Medical Negligence Cases*. For that one, I wrote about 98% of the trial part of the book, and Dr. Wecht wrote the medical sections. Stanley, for obvious reason, got top billing, and the books were well received by the legal community.

Much of Stanley's legal work was now related to corporate matters, which was a nice change from the pressures of the court room. Yet he just couldn't get that adversarial energy out of his blood. In late 1987 he was off to Charlottesville, Virginia, to try a two-week breach of contract construction case.

In 1988, Stanley returned to Pittsburgh. He was engaged to represent the son of a prominent Pittsburgh lawyer who had been charged with the murder of another well-known attorney's nephew. It was clear that Lawyer No. 1's son had shot Lawyer No. 2's nephew, but it was much less certain that the shooting constituted murder. The newspapers ran wild, but Stanley knew his client was ill. Just before trial in early 1989, Stanley and co-counsel George Mahfood reached a plea bargain with the prosecution. The 24-year-old young man would spend 7-15 years in a state mental hospital. Sometimes the best a criminal lawyer can do for a client is to keep him or her out of prison, and make sure they get the help they need.

About the same time, a lady from the mid-west who had been a juror on one of Stanley's trials in Ohio many years before, wrote a letter. She addressed it simply to "Stanley in West Virginia." No last name. No address, or even town for that matter. The post office delivered it to my Charleston office. The content isn't relevant, but the fact that it was delivered is amazing. Stanley, with a sense of humor as enormous as his personality and his earned right to a little ego, had new business cards printed. They were completely blank except for large letters on one side that said only "STANLEY." With a twinkle in his eye, he would point out that this is all the President or the Queen would need. Naturally, he was kidding. At least a little, I think, but how he loved to hand them out.

1990 brought Stanley another high-profile client, but this time it wasn't a politician seeking help, but his wife. Dee Kessel was probably the most admired woman in West Virginia. Born in 1943, she was the daughter of a judge, had earned a music degree in college and a Ph.D. in Education, and anyone who met her knew right away she was just an all-around nice person. She was beautiful, too, and stood almost 6 feet tall in heels. In 1964, Dee was crowned Miss West Virginia. To the astonishment of everyone in love with Dee in West Virginia, including my 12-year-old self, she was chosen as "only" the 2nd runner up in the Miss America Competition. We had all been sure she was a shoe-in for that crown.

In 1965, Dee married handsome Gaston Caperton, a successful insurance executive and soon-to-be Governor, and together they parented two good-looking and accomplished sons. I ran into Gaston (known as "Gat") at many business functions and restaurants in the 1980's on a regular basis, and knew him to be a good guy as well.

As happens too often, perhaps, things went awry, and just before Gaston was elected Governor in 1990, the couple decided to divorce. Besides the usual family court complaints, this case involved some allegations of fraud in an amount of over $10,000,000. Stanley had represented many rich and/or powerful women in divorce matters over the years, and Dee engaged him to represent her interests here. I did not handle divorce cases, but got to know Dee during her many visits to my office to meet with Stanley.

After a pretty good battle, the case was confidentially settled behind closed doors. The newspapers wanted quotes, of course, and Stanley simply told them that all was over, he could not disclose the terms of settlement, but everyone, he said, was extremely happy. Dee followed with a statement that hit the papers nationwide, "Underline 'extremely'."

Governor Caperton had a sense of humor, too. The following year he won the West Virginia Trial Lawyers Association Public Servant of the Year Award for his work on behalf of the citizens of West Virginia. As Chair of the Awards Committee, I presented his award at a gala luncheon sponsored by my firm, Preiser Law Offices. Of course, everyone knew about the divorce. As the Governor accepted the award from me, he mischievously looked at the audience and said, "I see the Preisers are sponsoring this. Don't believe it. It's my money."

Stanley was back in Pittsburgh in late 1990 representing Rocco Viola, assistant to a racketeer who was described as the second most powerful man in the Pittsburgh La Cosa Nostra. We will call him Mr. Jones. Viola had been charged with money laundering. The prosecution offered evidence that Viola payed Mr. Jones a "ghost salary" as an employee of Viola's food company, even though Jones never did any actual work there. The case looked solid for the Government, but Stanley had devised a defense that as long as Viola actually paid Mr. Jones the money, and as long as he filed all the appropriate papers and withheld the required taxes, there was no statute requiring the recipient employee to ever actually come to work.

Apparently, Mr. Viola was unhappy with Stanley's bill. He fired Stanley mid case and engaged a suburban practitioner named Richard Rosenswieg to initiate a fee dispute resolution process with the Allegheny County Bar Association. In his dispute resolution filing, Rosenswieg claimed, among other things, that Stanley was incompetent and overcharged for his legal services.

Stanley was so offended that he hired Howard Specter to sue Rosenswieg for defamation. Rosenswieg defended himself, not by reiterating that the charges were true, but by claiming that technically a lawyer had complete privilege to say what s/he wants in a judicial proceeding, which he claimed this was. The case procured a landmark opinion from the Pennsylvania Supreme Court, which held that fee dispute filings are not judicial proceedings, and accordingly, defamatory statements made in those filings were actionable.

Of course, no one was ever going to be able to prove that Stanley was an incompetent attorney. Knowing he was done for, Rosenswieg penned a widely circulated, three-page abject apology. According to Gregg Rosen, who read the document, Rosenswieg retracted everything he said, waxed eloquent about Stanley and his reputation for honesty, integrity and billing, and apologized profusely over and over again. Stanley was much more concerned about his reputation than he was about extracting a monetary penalty from the offending parties.

However, when Stanley subsequently sued Viola for his unpaid fees, the Rosenswieg letter, in a large understatement, came in pretty handy.

Never timelier than today, perhaps, is how one defines democracy – not just technically, but what it should really mean under the Constitution. As a child of an immigrant, and one who always tried to protect the weak, Stanley's well-grounded philosophy about America was espoused thusly, "Democracy means rule by the majority, but only while respecting the rights of the minority."

I mentioned earlier that Stanley had handled at least one matter in the early 1990's involving Donald Trump. When Trump became highly visible in the new millennium, Stanley was free in his vocal opinion of the man. Had Stanley been alive in 2016, he would have added a powerful and persuasive voice against voting for someone of Trump's ilk, and he would have been appalled at what the justice system has become, and at the almost total loss of judicial independence.

Joyce and Stanley did not tend to advertise this, but they were extremely generous when it came to worthy causes. They regularly gave large sums to cancer research, the United Way, the Heart Fund, the Federated Charities (sort of a Jewish United Way that distributes funds where needed most at any given time), their Synagogue, and to almost any organization or individual that had a legitimate fundraising drive or need. They also chaired a number of drives and fundraising dinners, and were honored for their efforts by more than one group.

After Stanley's death, my mother became a bit more of a homebody than she had been when her energetic husband always had something he wanted to do, or somewhere he wanted to go. One of the few activities she seemed to enjoy were luncheons or teas with those who contributed to the same major charities as she.

When my mother died, I served as the personal representative of her estate. Sara and I would go to her house almost daily to perform the usual personal representative tasks, which included checking the mail, paying expenses, etc. Upon opening Mom's checkbook, we were literally flabbergasted to see that she supported about 40 charities in addition to the ones about which people already knew. It's not as if Mom was writing thousand-dollar checks to each cause, but a $20-$25 check to each of about 25 different organizations every month, and perhaps 15 or so others once a year. If she received a request, she heeded the call. We always knew of Stanley's and Joyce's generous hearts, but it amazed us that these people we knew better than anyone else had likely donated in this manner for 60 years – we just didn't know it. But I digress.

Worrell Enterprises owned a string of small newspapers, and in 1971 purchased the respected *Daily Progress* in Charlottesville. Tom Worrell moved his home and headquarters to this urbane city (home of the University of Virginia), and Stanley handled litigation issues for the media group for many years.

From 1992-1995 the paper was in a battle with the realtors of the region who had, according to the suit filed by Stanley and Worrell's in-house counsel, banded together to illegally boycott all real estate advertising in the *Progress*. The realtors had founded a magazine of their own, and their trade association pressured all members to limit their advertising to that publication. Worrell sued the Association and various realtors who led the boycott, seeking $52,000,000 in damages. This case was one of the centerpieces of the news throughout the time the suit was pending. The parties resolved their dispute in 1995, and the Worrell group sold their media holdings soon after.

It was during these years that Stanley decided to give up the frequent travel north and focus his energies on matters in Florida. He won the Presidency of Boca Grove, the community where he lived. The residents of this country club were a very wealthy mix of successful, still working younger folks in their 40's and early 50's, plus older retirees, many of whom used the Club for a second home in the winter. Stanley, always youthful, fit into both categories. His expertise and broad knowledge, as well as his and Joyce's shared charisma, made them particular favorites of the younger set. Despite Stanley's occasional "complaint" about being the chief of 200 other chiefs, he enjoyed a year at the helm marked by the continued good fortune of the Club.

Yet the law would not release its grip on Stanley. He missed it. He relished reading about it, thinking about it, and discussing it. By this time, I was about 47 years old and close to retirement. Though some might describe my legal career as significant, I wanted something else while still young. My future, non-legal aspirations, were in activities such as food and wine journalism, publishing a wine magazine, owning a winery, and investing in Broadway shows. Stanley, unfortunately, lost a sounding board. I simply wasn't keeping up with what was transpiring in the legal world. Naturally, he couldn't understand how I could walk away.

Stanley's solution was to increase his involvement with the two firms to which he served as "Of Counsel," and to open his doors for lawyers nationwide to come and consult. It was not unusual after that to see people in his den, or waiting their turn in the living room to see him. His most frequent visitor was John Romano, who owned, and still owns, one of the best trial firms in Florida. He had already been close to the Preiser family for over 20 years.

John and Stanley handled numerous cases together over a better than ten-year period – Stanley advising and bringing in some of the business, and John doing his usual stellar work in depositions and the courtroom. However, I think it was the opportunity to have a top legal brain like John to talk to almost every day that most enthralled Stanley and kept him alert.

Here is how John tells it:

> *I first met Stanley Preiser in the Spring of 1976. He was one of the featured speakers on a trial advocacy seminar event for "J.A.G." officers. It was a truly extraordinary event. Speakers included Stanley Preiser, Richard "Racehorse" Haynes, Henry Rothblatt, F. Lee Bailey and more. It was a 3-day event – an event where I remember Stanley Preiser standing out as he was the lawyer who tried all the cases – murder, medical malpractice, product defect, negligent security, divorce, eminent domain, defamation of character and more. Stanley was indeed the total package.*
>
> *The day I met him was the first time I saw him speak – a day I will remember in such a positive way forever! It is true that Stanley Preiser provided us with a most remarkable, inspirational and motivational lecture on courtroom advocacy. Yet – what I remember the most – and it is as if it were yesterday – he was so open, warm and engaging with us that evening as we had a special event over at the Officer's Club at Camp LeJeune. He and*

many of the others were telling us war stories – giving us advice – sharing wisdom – opening our eyes to a new way of thinking as young advocates. It was in many respects a day (and an event) that changed my entire life, career, and outlook as a lawyer – mostly because of what I saw in Stanley Preiser.

As soon as I moved into civilian private practice out of West Palm Beach, I began to work with Stanley and Monty Preiser and their great law firm in Charleston, West Virginia. We gave lecture presentations together all over America. We planned and organized educational events together. We handled cases and injury related projects together. We were engaged in fundraising together State by State for every kind of cause imaginable relating to the tort system and the work we do as plaintiffs' trial lawyers. As the bond grew with Stanley and Monty, so grew the relationship and the friendship.

Stanley was also working with another firm, but advising more on corporate matters for them while handling some high-income divorce work. The senior partner at that firm, Howard Weiss, lived two doors away from Stanley and the two of them would often spend an hour or more walking the community and talking law. No matter how prominent Howard became in the legal community, he always treated Stanley as a mentor,

In 1998, Stanley and Joyce threw a blow-out to end all blow-outs in honor of their 50th wedding anniversary. Family, friends, and colleagues descended from all over the country on the club at Boca Grove for a black-tie evening of dinner, dancing, and professional entertainment in the form of a New York ventriloquist, and what else but the best Jolson impersonator of the day.

The time around 1995-2005 were good years for Stanley and

Joyce. They doted on both teen-age grandchildren, who, in turn, visited their grandparents often. They continued to enjoy the amenities of club living, and their legions of friends, and add: including Bob and Thelma Levine, Art and Sheila Driben, and Don and Candy Slavin. They had lost close neighbors Art and Hannah Druckman a few years before. Indeed, they were so popular it was difficult for Sara and me to get through a meal with them in the Boca Grove dining room because of all the people who would stop at the table to chat. Stanley was able to play golf, pontificate with Howard, have chats with John, and socialize with Sara and me. They frequently entertained, traveled to life style events of their friends and relatives, and their health was reasonably good.

There was a small setback in 2002, however. At a wedding in Ft. Lauderdale Stanley became disoriented and showed all the symptoms of congestive heart failure. He was rushed to the hospital where he recovered relatively quickly. However, he made it known he would undergo no more heart surgery there, or anywhere. He was 75 and would not go through that hell again.

Over the next 2-3 years Stanley finally began to really take it easy. People were, however, not about to stop coming to the house to see him and ask his advice, but that was elixir for Stanley – he loved it. John Romano was there often. So was Stanley's great friend Robert Volpe, his and the family's financial advisor. We all owe Robert more than we can say for his wise counsel, not only while Dad was alive, but continuing until this day.

For a man who knew so much about so many things, the extent of Dad's lack of knowledge about certain topics was ironic. He was either an expert in a subject because he had handled a case about it, incredibly well informed because he took an interest in a subject and remembered all he read, or entirely clueless if the topic did not interest him. He had simply never had the time for things he considered unimportant. Fred Fahrenz, now deceased, of the firm when it was Preiser and Wilson, was one of Stanley's best second chairs. He used to kid Dad about his funny responses to questions involving pop culture references.

For example, when Stanley received a call to represent the Grand Funk Railroad, he asked with all sincerity, "Is that a passenger or freight line?" During the Cyril Wecht trial, when Dr. Wecht said Mean Joe Greene and Willie Stargell would testify as character witnesses, Stanley had no idea who those professional sports icons were. This tendency continued into semi-retirement. My mother wanted Dad to work crossword puzzles with her, which was something she loved to do. She quickly saw the futility in that when Stanley could not fill in the four letters to the clue for 1-Across — "Alan ___ of M*A*S*H." From then on, Joyce turned to her granddaughter for team crossword solving. Stanley's concentration would thereafter center on law, golf, and family.

In 2006, fortunes changed dramatically. Stanley was advised that he needed another heart surgery, and this one would be tricky – there was only a 50% chance of survival, and no one knew, if he did live, how long he would have. If he declined the surgery, he would probably not see the end of the year, and life quality would be limited. It was a highly troublesome decision for Dad. Given his memory of his previous procedure, he did not want to go through another surgery at almost 80, and he had, in fact, vowed to have no more.

Ultimately, his love of life, and his belief that his family needed him for a while longer, persuaded him to consent. It was a sophisticated procedure, and his non-interventional cardiologist, Seth Baum, searched out the man reputed to be the best heart surgeon at the Cleveland Clinic in Cleveland, Ohio. The surgery was scheduled for mid-December of 2006.

The operation took over eight gut wrenching hours, and when it was over, the surgeon said it went well. We were naturally relieved. Dad was moved to Cardiac ICU, where it was expected he would recuperate for a day or so before moving to ICU, and then up to a room. But something went wrong. He was not in a coma, but he did not awaken for 5 days.

And we were having trouble getting answers. Cardiac ICU rotated its staff and doctors every three days, so someone who began a shift three days after Dad's surgery had no idea what had been going on. The surgeon himself had effectively disappeared, leaving me to discuss Dad's condition with a first-year resident who, while it might sound odd, did not know as much medicine as I did from my many years of medical litigation.

Finally, on December 24th I asked Dr. Baum to please come from Florida to see Dad. Seth came immediately. In just a few moments, he determined that Stanley was being given the wrong medicine and suggested alternative treatment. It worked, and a couple of days later Dad was transferred to a regular room, was at least semi-alert, and we were all encouraged.

The next day I insisted on reviewing Dad's medical chart and noted an infection that was not being treated. That was enough for me. I arranged for a private hospital jet, Dr. Baum arranged for a bed and consultations at the Boca Regional Hospital, and we flew Dad home. Within the week he was close to his old self except that temporarily he could not speak well or eat solid food because of the extended intubation period.

Soon, however, he was home and recovering fully. By about September of 2007 he looked and felt terrific. He was able to play golf, return to partying, and, in effect, live almost his normal life.

We considered filing what would have been a solid malpractice suit against the Clinic and Dad's surgeon, but for many reasons, including Dad's reticence to spend his next few years dealing with the litigation, we passed.

Stanley enjoyed a couple of years of good health and good times, and then two events occurred in 2009 that helped confirm that the decision he made two years before to in fact undergo the surgery was the correct one.

In January, he hosted another large party, this time in honor of Joyce's 80th birthday. It was a sweet event held at *Arturo's Ristorante* in Boca, the go-to restaurant for Preiser family milestones, and it was doubly satisfying because we never thought Dad would ever look so healthy, and be in such command, again. Sadly, not long after that event his heart began to show its compromise. Dad needed a portable oxygen unit to be comfortable. But nothing was going to keep him away from his next big upcoming date in Las Vegas.

The American Trial Lawyers Association (a separate organization from the old ATLA and the new AAJ) was inducting its first ten trial lawyers into its Hall of Fame in March of 2009. The list was meant to include the best and most influential trial lawyers in the almost 230-year history of American jurisprudence. Included were John Adams, Clarence Darrow, Melvin Belli, Gerald Spence, Morris Dees, Bobby Lee Cook, Fred Levin, Johnny Cochran, Thurgood Marshall ... and Stanley E. Preiser, born a little over 81 years before in Charleston, West Virginia.

The induction was a highlight of Dad's life, which he had dedicated to justice and how to achieve it. Gregg Rosen wrote:

> *Stanley was the greatest teacher of law I met in more than 40 years of my practice. First and foremost, he taught me that*

the practice of law is an honorable profession and that lawyers should be proud. He disliked so called "lawyer" jokes because they demeaned his cherished calling. He believed that the law not only is a noble profession, but a necessary one. He proudly displayed on his "wall of fame" at home a framed version of the poem written by German Pastor Martin Niemöller about the price of cowardice that is quoted at the U.S. Holocaust Museum:

> **First they came for the Socialists, and I did not speak out –**
> **Because I was not a Socialist.**
> **Then they came for the Trade Unionists, and I did not speak out -**
> **Because I was not a Trade Unionist.**
> **Then they came for the Jews, and I did not speak out -**
> **Because I was not a Jew.**
> **Then they came for me - and there was no one left to speak for me.**

Stanley was the one who would speak for the oppressed, the victims of government overreach and the dispossessed, but usually for a fee. Stanley instilled in me the belief that lawyers should not be shy about charging fees. It was not ignoble to do so. At the same time, Stanley was also the most honest and ethical lawyer I ever met. I always joked, and still do, that Stanley practiced law with a law book in one hand and a copy of the Rules of Professional Responsibility (now typically known as the Rules of Professional Conduct) in the other. In the zeal of his advocacy, Stanley was not afraid to approach the boundary of ethical conduct, but he never crossed it.

Stanley was indeed a stickler about truth, not just because honor and the legal system demanded it, but because one could face all sorts of trouble otherwise. One evening, after a particularly acrimonious discussion with some associates about how some evidence would be presented, I heard Stanley say to them what he had been saying to me since I first thought about law school, and what he said to all his colleagues: "If someone has to go to jail, make sure it is your client, and not you."

The Hall of Fame induction was, for all practical purposes, the end, and a fitting one. From that Stanley went steadily downhill. He began living a life requiring constant and total care, which we all knew he did not wish to continue. Fortunately, his pain was controlled, and his last cognizant words to each of his family were to take care of the others – and, especially, to take care of Joyce. He passed away reasonably peacefully on December 17, 2009, at 82 years of age.

I hope that I have done justice to Stanley's extraordinary life in this work. And I thank Sara for her unending proof reading and thoughts, and my daughter Blair for her masterful editing. And I hope people will enjoy reading about this unique personality. But no matter the biography's reception, the endeavor has served to bring us all closer to Dad again, and that is worth everything.

WHEN THE FIGHT WAS OVER

Epilogue

I hope my eulogy to my father serves as an appropriate ending to this biography. I'm sure the reader has noticed the 15 Rounds, one of the usual lengths of a heavyweight boxing match. The title for this Epilogue seemed, then, to write itself. And now that you know so much about Stanley Preiser, I think the eulogy will have more meaning.

December 21, 2009: Boca Raton, Florida, by Monty Preiser

As you might suspect, my Dad, the world's ultimate planner and preparer, left written directions for this very day. What stands out in these pages is his fervent wish that neither this day, nor his death in general, be a time for sadness. He believed life should go on, and those who cared about him should not be overcome with grief and sorrow. That is how he lived – full of life and always looking toward tomorrow - and that is what he wished for all of us.

I don't think Dad ever thought he would make it through his 60's, much less into his 80's. In his younger years his drive for professional success found him working all night at least twice a week. Couple that with 3 packs of cigarettes and a half dozen cigars a day, and then sprinkle in a few large pepperoni pizzas weekly and good dose of alcohol on the weekends, and you had a recipe for an early death.

In fact, in 1967 some of his good friends gave him an engraved plaque - a sort of commendation for the achievement of actually reaching 40.

But fortunately, using that incredible discipline of his, one night he stopped smoking —- cold turkey. And that decision, along with an extra reason for living in the then recent birth of his grand-daughter Blair, who he adored from her first breath, helped pull him through a serious heart attack in early 1982. And from there until two years ago when his heart finally betrayed him permanently, he was, thanks primarily to his superb doctor and even better friend Seth Baum, a relatively healthy guy living a life that was admired by all.

Nevertheless, Dad made sure his family was prepared for his death, even going so far as to buy the caskets, choose his pall bearers, buy his burial plots, make sure Rabbi Urecki would be able to officiate, and arrange the music and beverages for after this service, which, surprise, will have Al Jolson singing, accompanied by fine wine and spirits. With a bit of humor, I can relate to you now that this stage direction of Dad's became quite a pain for his family. He lived so much longer than he thought he would that for years we had to take notes on the friends du jour, who the pallbearers would be (they changed every 3 years or so depending on who was still young enough to serve), etc., etc. But this was Stanley Preiser at his best – trying to take the burden off his family, as he did for countless friends, family members, and clients over five decades.

However, as I alluded to, it all caught up with him in the past two years, and though he had a relatively pain free six months during this time, for the past 7 months or so he was not comfortable, or able to really enjoy living. But two years of life is two years of life.

In some of our last conversations, Dad came to recognize his good fortune in being able to see Blair graduate law school and become a valued member of one of the world's great firms. He was able to see, and <u>em</u>cee, his beloved wife Joyce's 80th birthday party. He was overjoyed that my sister Terri showed such courage and resiliency in overcoming a serious injury to her arm. He was able to see his grandson Justin help establish a nationally recognized magazine and become engaged to a lovely young lady, Stacy Long. And he was able to be in Las Vegas for his induction into the American Trial Lawyers Hall of Fame with the likes of Johnny Cochran, Justice Thurgood Marshall, and Clarence Darrow. As an aside, Dad was pretty happy to be the one member of that group not getting the award posthumously.

Some of you present never had the opportunity to know my Dad when he was strong and robust, which he was for most of his life, and for which he was most proud. He was an excellent physical specimen who into his 70's would still invite you to try out a punch to the stomach. But it was his mind that enthralled and amazed most people.

- He could recall names of cases and their holdings from 50 years ago.
- He could try any kind of litigation since he could easily and quickly learn medicine, mechanical engineering, tax law, banking procedures, pathology, aeronautics, ballistics, or anything else.
- And his imagination and creativity won many a case. I remember he would often say to me that "Anyone can lose a case, but it takes a truly dedicated lawyer to win them." He

would then ask to be left alone when he would, as he called it, simply "cerebrate," and figure out a way to win, which he did (and this is not empty hyperbole) perhaps more often than any other trial lawyer in history.

There were so many people in awe of Dad. But what he really enjoyed was a good debate or discussion with friends who allowed him to be himself, and who had superior minds themselves – like a Cyril Wecht, a Howard Specter, a Tom Worrell, a John Romano, a Robert Volpe, a Gregg Rosen, a Richard Hailey, a Mary Beth Ramey, a George Mahfood, or an Alvin Preiser. He loved a good verbal joust with long-time friends and family he respected – like from his late brothers in law Eddie Kerman, and Lionel Garner, his brother in law Si Wolf, his nephew Douglas Preiser, former associate Trigg Salsbery, and his Boca Grove close pals. And he loved loyal friends, some of whom stayed in close touch with Dad during his waning months, such as Jim Humphries and Harry Deitzler.

In fact, I know of few people who inspired as much loyalty as did Stanley, and even fewer who gave of themselves to the extent that he did every day of his life. There are, and were, literally hundreds of family members, friends, and clients who owe vast debts of gratitude to Dad for his help in the most trying of times, as well as his continued friendship and counsel as the years went on. Having Stanley Preiser on your side was better than an Allstate Insurance policy.

For my sister and myself, other benefits were particularly advantageous. From an early time in our lives, education was stressed. Terri and I were invited to learn a new word every day to present to the family at the dinner table (where high economics were taught since we earned a dime per word). Dad took me to my first baseball games - minor league in Charleston, WV, and then to a Pittsburgh Pirates doubleheader with the Cardinals where, through his contacts, I sat with Stan Musial and Roberto Clemente in between games. How many kids can make that claim? Dad taught me to play football, as he had been an all-state lineman at Charleston High and a possible college player at Virginia before blowing a knee. In fact, I still throw a pretty spiral. And he first took me to see West Virginia play Pitt when I was but 12 years old, establishing for me a lifelong love of the Mountaineers, and a feeling for Pitt I won't mention because we have so many esteemed Pittsburghers in attendance today. But they understand.

It was harder for a father to do so much with a young daughter 45-50 years ago, but in an effort to keep a 4-year-old Terri quiet, he once made a promise to buy her a horse when she turned six. He thought she would forget. She didn't. So into the family came Lady Gayle, a horse of questionable worth who became a local champion. And thus began Dad and Terri's careers in the horse business (he as a stable owner and sometimes horse show and rodeo producer, and she as a rider). It was in this arena where the two of them could bond.

Sports, dinners, horses - it seemed to us Dad was always around. But the reality as we now know it is that he wasn't there as much as we remember because his work was so time consuming.

However, to leave us with that illusion of participation means that the time Dad did spend with us had to be of great quality.

Of course, it isn't at issue that Dad outworked all other lawyers and became as famous to his legal brethren as those names you know so well because they employed high power PR firms, such as Gerry Spence, Mel Belli, Lee Bailey, Johnny Cochran, and all the others who handled most of the important cases of those decades. And when these gentlemen needed help (there were no women trial lawyers of high fame in those days) - when these lawyers needed help they often called on Dad.

So growing up as Stanley's children provided Terri and me far more benefit than problem in most every aspect, from ethical teaching to education, from family history to financial stability, and in support for all endeavors, including for Sara and me the transition from lawyer and mother to wine writers/magazine publishers (for which approval Dad only gave once he finally came to Napa and saw we were serious, and not just drinking wine all day).

Now, Mom, we know Dad missed something important to Terri and me. It's a good thing you were there to instill in us our great love of the arts and music, which have been such vital parts of our lives. I'm also grateful for something just as notable - that you were there to insist Dad pay me a fair (OK, maybe a bit more than fair) salary when I first came to work, other members of the firm notwithstanding. I was, after all, his son. To a mother a little extra for HER son seemed fair. Not surprisingly, it did to me too.

The two most important things about life, according to Dad, are that people should do their best, and that their primary responsibility should be their family.

Stanley Preiser received an A+ in achieving these goals, the same scores he received, as a matter of fact, in most of his law school classes, where he graduated with the highest grades ever from the University of Louisville law school. In reaching his goals, he left behind a part of him in each of his children and grandchildren.

In his grandson Justin he left great business acumen and an ability to see the world as it really is.

In his granddaughter Blair he left a stellar legal mind and apparently (though Sara and I had hoped differently) a love of the court room.

In his daughter Terri he left his idealism that there was always something over the next horizon that would add to the enjoyment of many.

For his daughter Sara (for he never called her his daughter in law) he left the memories of having a father, and a pretty great one at that. You see, her Dad had died when she was too young to really remember much about him, and she had over 31 years of Stanley in her life.

But the story that tells it all as to Sara and Dad's relationship is that when Sara and I got married Dad promised Sara's mother that he would always take care of Sara. Just before the time came when he could no longer hold a conversation, Dad took Sara aside and told her he thought he had held up the promise he made to her mother, and now he asked for one from Sara - to take care of Joyce.

And as for what Dad primarily left me, well, if I had to choose one thing, I think watching him for 50 years instilled in me a hatred of bullies, in whatever form.

- I watched him take on insurance companies who refused to pay contracted for funds to people on disability.
- I watched him take on, and take down, judges who bullied lawyers because of their sex or religion.
- I watched him take on the Federal Government in the form of U.S. Attorneys, IRS agents, and special agents, who all thought they had a free run at whomever they indicted or threatened to indict.
- I watched him write one the broadest and first open housing laws in the U.S. because he hated the treatment suffered by the African American as early as the mid 60's.
- And I saw him come to the aid of the man or woman on the

street who had little materially, but was being taken advantage of by nothing more than a local store that sold him or her a bum product, and would not take it back.

It didn't matter how rich or poor someone was – if their cause was just, Dad was their champion, no matter how powerful or influential the bully.

As most of you know, Dad had become a shadow of himself in these last months. He could not breathe without serious levels of oxygen, he could no longer walk without help, his voice was gone, and he was ultimately house bound. He finally did not really want people to see him. Yet his love for his family was still apparent. Every time I came to the house, he would ask in a raspy voice, "What's new?" which was his code for, "Can I help you with anything?" And he always wanted to hold Mom's hand, and perked up when she gave him a kiss. That was beautiful . . .

But, chronic congestive heart failure is not a pretty thing. Oh that Fickle Heart. I have thought it a paradox that the man with the finest heart of anyone I knew should come to his end because that heart had failed him. But one of the country's best lawyers, and one of my Dad's best friends, Gary Gober of Nashville, probably put it best when I mentioned this irony. He said that Stanley's heart failed "because he gave so much of it to so many different people and causes." I think he is right.

My family thanks all of you for coming today. Dad would have liked your being here as he did not think many people would show up. They came, Dad, and but for the horrible eastern weather other good friends would have been here as well.

We'll all miss you Dad. I'll miss you more than I ever told you. But you are at peace, and for that we are all grateful. No one loved his family more than you. . . and we love you – that you knew, and I believe still know.

We don't have a glass in hand as we sit here, but my father's toast was always the same – to Victory, for he believed that when you have victory you have it all. So, here's to you Dad as you prepare that next case for whomever needs help up there.

To Victory !!

ACKNOWLEDGMENTS

I have tried to be certain everything in this biography was backed up in time and fact by newspaper accounts, personal documents, or information gathered from a first source. Some of the times may be off a bit chronologically, but I don't think that is relevant in any way to story or goal. Likewise, I may have taken a little poetic license here and there, but, again, I don't believe it affected the accuracy of anything being written.

If there are episodes or commentary about other people that the reader thinks should have been included herein, the decision to omit that information, or the failure to remember it, is solely my responsibility. And while this work is about Stanley Preiser, because I was his son and legal colleague, naturally I often serve as a first source, or as a relevant part of a story. Those instances of inclusion, too, were choices that I made.

Strange as it may seem, I would never have had the time, or perhaps more accurately, *made* the time, necessary to write a 250-page biography unless I had been in some way confined to my home. This was of course during the horrific late winter, spring, and (as of the time of writing) summer months of 2020, when more than 200,000 people in this country gave their lives – many because our Government was unprepared to fight the virus, ignored the dangers at first, and did not know what to do once the problem was unmanageable.

Therefore, I want to dedicate this work in part to the families who lost loved ones and friends, to those who were unable to combat this scourge, and to the valiant front-line health care givers. May we soon recover and never go through this again.

There are a number of others, some no longer with us, that I would like to remember. They are courageous experts who risked informal censure and criticism from their colleagues for speaking out on behalf of those injured by dangerous products or poor medical care. They include Dr. Bob Brenner, Dr. Yale Koskoff, Dr. Lee Levitt, Dr. Robert Lott, Dr. Robert Nugent, Dr. Melvyn Ravitz, Dr. Stephen Smith, Dr. Cyril Wecht, and Dr. Saul Weinstein.

One person to whom I owe much of any personal success I may have had, is our friend Jeanne Classé, a lawyer and noted *professeur* of French. She knows why. And I mention Ted Kanner, who has been a constant friend for over a half century, and Robert Volpe, whose advice to our family has been invaluable.

I also would like to dedicate this book to my beautiful wife of 42 years, Sara Preiser, who loved my father as I did, and was a bedrock of good sense as she proofread my memories. This book would not have been completed without her.

My thanks to our daughter, Blair Preiser Wolfson of Pittsburgh, who is truly an exceptional writer and lawyer. Her skills in these areas were vital. Also, to our wonderful son, Justin, who edits our magazine, runs our winery in Napa, is now our winemaker, and who picked up all of the slack. Thanks to Gregg Rosen, who not only helped with editing, but provided much insight. And, thanks and love to Howard and Elaine Specter, to whom I have been able to turn for advice about anything since the loss of my father. No one outside our immediate family could be more important to us.

Along those lines, it is my hope that our grandchildren Caden and Eliana Wolfson will someday find great joy in this work about their great-grandfather. They, and all of us, have a chance to read about Dad's last 25 years because of the great work of his Charleston friend and doctor Harold Selinger, who brought Dad back to life after his 1984 heart attack, and, along with another friend and cardiologist, Boca's Seth Baum, helped make sure Stanley stayed around.

Finally, but not insignificant in any way, I thank family, friends, and colleagues for sharing, and making me recall, stories about my Dad. He certainly left a lot of great memories for legions of people. These include Barbara (Fleisher) Allen, Judge Duke Bloom, Bill Druckman, Michael Farrell, Lee Forb, David Fryson, Rosaria Gismondi, Richard Hailey, Judy Wilson Hill, Ted Kanner, George Mahfood, Bill Parsons, Craig Pearlman, Alvin Preiser, Mary Beth Ramey, John Romano, Gregg Rosen, Hope Rosenburg, Elaine Specter, Howard Specter, David Stuart, Rabbi Victor Urecki, Beth White, and Judge Joe Zak. Their contributions were invaluable.

To Victory !

Monty Preiser
Boynton Beach, FL
Summer/Fall 2020

ABOUT THE AUTHOR

Attorney Monty Preiser and his wife Sara Preiser reside full time in Palm Beach County, Florida, yet divide their time between Florida and Napa, where they have a second home and spend their time visiting wineries, studying wines, publishing a well-known guide, and owning a boutique winery.

Prior to wading full time into the wine industry, Monty was a trial lawyer who specialized in representing young children injured by vaccines and other medications. He also litigated cases for the injured workforce against the makers of defective machines, as well as medical negligence cases of note that helped improve hospital and doctor care. He published three legal text books, and served as President of both the West Virginia and Southern Trial Lawyers Associations.

Writing about wines for over 25 years, the Preisers, along with their son Justin, publish the world's most comprehensive guide to Napa Valley wineries and restaurants titled, appropriately, *The Preiser Key*, in which they create and pen many informational and educational articles. The guides have received accolades as the best (or indispensable) from, among others, famed writer Jancis Robinson of the *Financial Times, Dine Magazine, msnbc.com, cnn.com,* and *Frommer's Guide.*

Over the years, Monty and Sara have served as wine columnists and wine editors for numerous magazines and trade publications throughout the country. They were the principal wine writers for one of the Internet's largest travel sites, and were regularly published by *Wine-On-Line-International.* They now write an international wine column and own Creative Professional Programs, a company devoted to continuing education for professionals in conjunction with fine wine & food instruction. They also co-own Shadowbox Cellars, which produces a number of premium wines. The Preisers enjoy cruising and have presented shipboard lectures to various cruise ship passengers, as well as taught at various Fortune 500 events.

INDEX

ed

,16